Will I Ever Feel Good Again?

WILL I EVER FEEL GOOD AGAIN?

WHEN YOU'RE OVERWHELMED BY GRIEF AND LOSS

Karen Dockrey

Fleming H. Revell
A Division of Baker Book House Co
Grand Rapids, Michigan 49516

© 1993 by Karen Dockrey

Published by Fleming H. Revell
a division of Baker Book House Company
P. O. Box 6287, Grand Rapids, MI 49516-6287

Printed in the United States of America

Library of Congress Cataloging-in-Publication Data

Dockrey, Karen, 1955–
    Will I ever feel good again : when you're overwhelmed by grief and loss
/ Karen Dockrey.
        p.   cm.
    ISBN 0-8007-5475-1
    1. Bereavement—Religious aspects—Christianity. 2. Consolation. I.
Title.
BV4905.2.D63   1993
248.8'6—dc20   93-31249

For Heidi

Contents

Find Hope in the Midst of Hurt

When death, disappointment, disease, disability, or divorce strikes, both you and those around you go through grief and guilt. You grieve for what you've lost. You feel guilty about what you wish you had done before the tragedy, what you might have done to prevent it, or what you may have done to cause it. You feel angry that this sad event has happened and wonder why it happened at all.

This book will help you explore your sad, guilty, angry, and confused feelings. You can discover why your feelings make sense and what to do about them. You can walk through your sadness and anger to the joy and peace on the other side. You can find forgiveness from guilt and freedom from regret. You can tap into God's power and let him help you find confidence to give good again. You can look toward the future, toward reunion with those who have died, and to the perfection that awaits you as a believer in Jesus Christ.

Grief and guilt are more like a tunnel than a wall or doorway. It takes time to move through them. As you move through the pain and darkness, keep your eyes on the light at the end of the tunnel, the light given by God himself. Choose to walk on through the tunnel and fully feel the pain, taking the hand of someone you care about. Only as you walk through the pain can you heal and experience full joy.

Guiding you through the grieving process, this book will help you share your feelings with God and also with other humans. You will discover answers to your questions, release from your fears, and hope for your future. No matter where you are in this walk from sadness to happiness, God is with you. You never have to walk the road alone.

> *Even though I walk through the valley of the shadow of death, I will fear no evil, for you [God] are with me; your rod and your staff, they comfort me.*
>
> *Psalm 23:4*

> *I will not leave you as orphans; I will come to you.*
>
> *John 14:18*

> *The LORD appeared to us in the past, saying: "I have loved you with an everlasting love; I have drawn you with loving-kindness. I will build you up again and you will be rebuilt . . . Again you will . . . go out to dance with the joyful."*
>
> *Jeremiah 31:3–4*

> *And God shall wipe away all tears from their eyes; and there shall be no more death, neither sorrow, nor crying, neither shall there be any more pain: for the former things are passed away.*
>
> *Revelation 21:4 KJV*

This book is a guided journal. With a blend of text and response space, you can read about elements of grief and guilt and then record how you are experiencing or have experienced them. The book explores the nature of grief and guilt, the forms in which they come to us, and how to respond to them. You can respond to Scripture, stories, and others' reactions with writing, art, doodles, prayers, thoughts, or whatever expression is most comfortable for

10

you. As you read and respond, you discover that there is a path through the dark days—there is an end to pain. The book then becomes not only a help for the present crisis but also a record of a personal journey, an account you can reread when grief or guilt comes again.

My goal is to assure you that you can find and give happiness again, that despair is not your only choice, that there is a safe path through the pain. As you walk with God through grief, you can live as a healed, whole, and joyful person.

Two chapters at the end of the book enhance the usability of *Will I Ever Feel Good Again?* First, a giver's guide offers tips for walking with a friend through the grief process and for encouraging a friend to accept and live God's forgiveness of guilt. Second, a leader's guide offers suggestions for working through the book in a group and for developing the kind of love and mutual support that make healing possible.

CHAPTER 1

It Can't Be True!

SURVIVE THE SHOCK OF FINDING OUT

But is he dead?" asked Jerome.

"Of course he's dead," responded Casey. "That's what drowned means—death by water."

"But he can't be dead. I just saw him yesterday," insisted Jerome.

"Well, he is. The boat capsized and he didn't make it to shore. He was a good swimmer, but the tide was too strong. He had refused to wear a life jacket," explained Casey.

In a daze Jerome hung up the phone. *How could Karl be dead? How could somebody my age drown?*

Jerome's not crazy. He's shocked. Shock is the first reaction to death or other sad news. Jerome knows that drowned means dead, but he can't believe it yet. *No!* protest both his mind and his heart. *I don't want it to be true, so it can't be true.* The shock of tragedy and the drastic change tragedy demands make us want to fight against it, to declare it not so.

Jerome knows that people die and that some of those people are his age. But logic doesn't help much when he's upset about Karl's death. Jerome doesn't need to be pushed to accept reality. He simply needs time for it to sink in. He's heading into a painful but important experience called grief, the reviewing of and recovery from a sad experience.

Journaling Suggestions

Recall a time you felt shocked. Describe or draw your first reaction when you heard that someone important to you had died, when you were diagnosed with a serious illness or disability, or when you received other very sad news. What were your first thoughts? Your first actions?

Your first words?

Here are a few reactions other people experienced after a sudden shock. Describe or draw similar feelings you've had.

"I couldn't think."

"I coped by taking care of other people."

"The simplest tasks seemed confusing or hard."

"I kept thinking she'd walk in any minute."

What did other people do to help you? Describe any actions you liked, or would have liked.

What did people do that hurt? What do you wish they'd done instead?

Choose the Path That Leads Back to Happiness

Jerome's shock is the first step in a journey called grief. In the midst of his shock and sadness he finds it hard to believe he'll ever feel good again. But joy can and will come back to him. It won't, and shouldn't, come right away. But little by little sadness will heal and happiness will grow stronger. If Jerome denies or covers up his sad feelings, they will stay with him and emerge as anger, depression, or some other masked form. But if he moves on through his sadness, he'll find joy on the other side. This passage through the pain of loss to the happiness on the other side is what we call grief.

We frequently connect grief with the death of a friend or family member. But grief and mourning happen after any sad event, including:

* *diagnosis of a serious illness*
* *moving from one home to another, or a close friend moving away*
* *divorce*
* *an accident or hospitalization*
* *being cut from a sports team*
* *losing a contest, an election, or a job*
* *making a mistake*
* *doing poorly on a test, tryout, or competition*
* *a positive change, such as moving to middle school, high school, or college*
* *obstacles caused by a disability*
* *any disappointment.*

The more life-shaking the event, the longer the grief lasts. The shock, sadness, guilt, and anger of grief are godly and good reactions to tragic events. These feelings are not contradictory to Christianity—they are steps toward healing, steps toward feeling good again.

Ecclesiastes 3:1, 4 explains:

There is a time for everything, and a season for every activity under heaven . . . a time to weep and a time to laugh, a time to mourn and a time to dance.

To return to happiness, you must choose to walk through the sadness in whatever form it comes to you. Remember, if you refuse the journey through sadness, your pain will remain. Leave pain behind by walking on through it. Take God's hand as you walk, confident that he'll keep you safe. Know that eventually you'll feel good again.

Ride the Waves

Grief comes in waves. Some waves are flutters of sadness you barely feel. Other waves are so high and jolting you think they'll overpower you. But don't be afraid—there's always an end to the wave, and you can always ride it out. Recall Psalm 23:4 to assure you that goodness and love will follow your sadness. God will keep you from going under.

* The waves of grief come in types and in stages.
* The types and stages aren't always in order.
* Sometimes two or more waves come together.
* Some waves are easier to ride, but all can be ridden safely.
* Once one type of wave passes, it may come back again.

There are chapters in this book on each wave.

SHOCK   SADNESS   GUILT   ANGER   DEPRESSION   ACCEPTANCE

Shock

The first wave to come is shock. You hear the news and can hardly think about or believe it. Perhaps someone you care for deeply has died. Perhaps you've been diagnosed with a life-threatening illness. Perhaps a friend has been crippled in a horrible accident. The shock may last a minute, a day, or a week, depending on the severity of the experience. Jerome's shock lasted a weekend. When he returned to school without Karl, the reality of Karl's death hit home and hit hard.

People watching during the funeral said, "Jerome is taking it so well." Jerome wondered why he didn't feel like crying or why he didn't feel worse. In reality, he felt so deeply that his feeling circuits had overloaded and switched off. His emotions protected themselves from too much too fast.

One way we express shock is to name all the reasons why we can't accept what has happened. Jerome's reaction was, "But I just saw him yesterday!" Others say things like, "Nobody understands me like Dan. How can he move away?" or "I loved Grandmother so much. How will I go on without her?"

18

Sadness

The second wave to arrive is intense sadness. Depending on your personality, you may cry, sob, sigh, or just get quiet. The despair and loneliness seep into everything you do and think.

Jerome didn't do much crying during school, but his head felt thick and heavy. He couldn't concentrate, and his mind kept wandering to Karl. Jerome's steps were slow; the things that usually interested him held little appeal. He just felt empty inside. Some nights he stayed awake remembering. Other nights he slept hard and long.

Like Jerome, walk on through the sadness, one slow step at a time, until you pass through it. At home, Jerome reminisced, cried, laughed about old times, and cried some more. Just keep reminding yourself, "One more day, and then one more day. This excruciating sadness won't last forever, no matter how bad I feel right now." Don't try to make any big decisions when you're sad. And refuse to try suicide or other destructive actions—feeling nothing may seem better than feeling bad, but suicide allows no opportunity for feeling better. Just focus on making it for one more day.

Guilt

You may feel guilty for doing or not doing something with the one who has died, moved, or been disabled. "But I was going to tell him about Jesus," Jerome lamented. "We almost talked a couple times, but we never really got going. Will he go to hell?"

You may feel responsible (or you may actually be responsible) for the incident that paralyzed your friend. Casey wishes he had worn his life jacket and pushed Karl to wear one too; if Karl had worn a life jacket maybe he wouldn't have died.

Explore your guilt in chapter 3 to discover if it is true guilt or simply regret. Let God forgive your real guilt and heal your regret. Confessing to a friend often helps this process. Casey knows that Karl was ultimately responsible for his own actions but that his actions influenced Karl. Casey confessed his action to God and to Jerome. He vowed to wear his life jacket and car seat belt regularly. He didn't feel better automatically, but he healed day by day. Jerome confessed to Casey his neglect to share Jesus with Karl. Both talked about how hard it is to bring up spiritual matters. They thought of ways to do so with other friends.

Anger

You may feel angry at the doctors, at God, at yourself, even at the person who died or was injured. Talk with God and an understanding friend. God understands your anger and wants to heal you. Explore your anger in chapter 4.

Jerome became angry with Karl for not wearing his life jacket. *If you had worn your life jacket, Karl, you'd be alive today,* he fumed inwardly. *Why did you have to arrogantly assume you were invincible?* Jerome let the waves of anger come, and he rode each one out by thinking it through. Gradually each wave dissipated. Initially Jerome was so angry he felt like putting his fist through the wall. He chose to lift weights instead, directing his anger through his muscles.

Other feelings besides anger may come as well. You may dream about the one who died, or think you see him; you may imagine that you no longer have the disability. When my grandfather died I kept dreaming that he sat up in his casket and said, "Don't worry, I'm not really dead." I was so relieved. Then I woke up and reality hit again. Every bald man that came along reminded me of my grandfather, especially when I saw them from behind. Even years later bald people make me feel a little lonely for my grandaddy. Every time Jerome saw a car like Karl's, he did a double take.

In addition, you may feel you're coming down with whatever killed or injured your loved one. Jerome steered away from water sports for a while.

Depression

Depression and deep loneliness commonly occur a week or two after the funeral or crisis. Such deep sadness made Jerome wonder if he could go on without Karl, if anything

 would ever feel interesting or fun again. Explore your depression in chapters 5 through 7.

Depression can also come at significant times like birthdays and Christmas. After finally feeling happy again after your sad experience, you may be surprised to feel suddenly sad. A memory, a song, or even fatigue can cause this to happen. Jerome missed Karl on youth retreats because they had always shared a cabin. The trips just weren't the same without him.

Let other friends and family love you through this fragile time. Lean on God's arms, praying even when you don't have words to frame your prayers (see Romans 8:26–27).

Acceptance

Eventually you'll feel like yourself again. You'll become able to move on with life, comfortable with your memories. The only way to get to this point is to go through the sadness, guilt, anger, and depression. Jerome knew that no one would ever replace Karl and was glad Karl had been a part of his life. But he made other friends. He laughed again. Enjoyed life again. It wasn't that he quit missing Karl or was happy about Karl's death, but he was able to embrace life again. Examine how to do this in chapters 7 and 8.

Take Your Friend Along

You're never alone on your journey through sad times. No matter where you are in your walk from sadness to happiness, God is with you. No matter what wave is hitting you, God will hold your head above the water. Like a loyal friend, he stays by your side and never abandons you. He also provides family and friends to care for you. Think about Psalm 23:4 word by word, and doodle or describe your thoughts. Here are some ideas to get you started.

Even though	Nobody likes death or pain or other sad experiences. But these are a part of life on earth. When sadness comes, we have someone to turn to. So even though . . .
I walk through	Walking through sadness, frustration, and discouragement is no fun. Sometimes all we can do is put one foot in front of the other. As I walk through . . .
The valley of the shadow of death	Whether it involves my death, someone else's death, or an illness that threatens death . . .
I will fear no evil	There are two reasons we have no evil to fear: 1. *You [God] are with me.* Draw, describe, or doodle God's presence with you.

22

2. *Your rod and your staff, they comfort me.* A rod and staff are instruments of both defense and guidance. How might God's defense and guidance comfort you through sadness? Draw, describe, or doodle a symbol of God's comfort.

We can make it through the valley of the shadow of death because God will guide us safely all the way.

Surely goodness and love will follow me all the days of my life, and I will dwell in the house of the LORD forever.
Psalm 23:6

Draw or doodle your response to this promise.

Walk through the Tunnel

It may seem strange, but the best way back to happiness is right smack through the middle of sadness. Think of sadness as a tunnel—it's dark for a while, but soon the light shows at the end. And finally you're in that light. You never forget what's behind you, but you're ready to enjoy life again. That's grief. That's the path back to happiness.

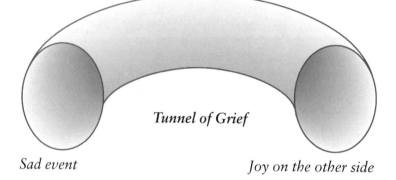

Tunnel of Grief

Sad event   *Joy on the other side*

On the tunnel above, draw or describe the event that brought your current or most recent sadness.

At the entrance to the tunnel, doodle or draw why you'd rather not think about this sad event, why you'd rather not go through it.

At the end of the tunnel, draw or describe how you'd like to feel when the sadness is over, when joy returns.

Now commit to travel through that tunnel, confident that the only way back to joy is through the grief. You need not fear the sadness, because you won't be alone. God and the family and friends he gives you will go with you on your journey. You can travel safely.

CHAPTER 2

I Miss Him So Much

WALK THROUGH SADNESS TO THE JOY ON THE OTHER SIDE

He was the only one who understood me. Now he's dead. All other adults laughed at my ideas or considered me childish. He never did. He saw the good. He made me feel important. He pointed out ways I was maturing and was able to spur me on in areas I was still weak. He didn't always agree with me, but at least he took me seriously. Because of that he could get me to think through my dangerous decisions or impulsive whims. He was the one adult who really seemed to like me just as I am," explained nineteen-year-old Melanie about her beloved grandfather. He had died suddenly while she was away at college, and Melanie felt she'd never find anyone else as wonderful as he was.

The first few days after his death she smiled and talked tearlessly with friends and family members who attended the funeral. As the shock melted away and reality began to sink in, tears came. Melanie felt sadder and more empty than she ever had before. She kept wishing it wasn't true. She hoped he'd walk into the room and sit in his familiar chair; she yearned for another of their long talks. When Melanie wasn't sad, she felt a kind of sick emptiness. She had never felt this bad.

Journaling Suggestions

Focus on your present sadness or another time you felt very sad. Circle and expand the description that most closely matches your sadness. Feel free to create a description of your own.

Heavy-hearted

Can't stop crying

Hope it's a bad dream

Don't like to think about it because it makes me sad

Cold inside, like I'll never warm up

No appetite for food or activity or friendship

Walk on through Your Sadness

The oppressiveness of grief can make you feel hopeless and helpless; the anguish and desolation seem like they will last forever. But they won't. Joy will come again. The Bible assures us:

Weeping may linger for the night, but joy comes with the morning.

Psalm 30:5b NRSV

Of course, the fact that joy will return doesn't mean you should never be sad. Quite to the contrary, taking time to be sad is important. Your sadness makes sense—the person you lost by death, divorce, circumstance, or distance *matters*. The sadness is a tribute to your love. Later on you'll feel like other forms of tribute:

* joy because of the good that person gave you
  * going on with life to show the confidence your friend or family member imparted
    * smiles over memories
      * happiness that reflects hope of reunion in heaven.

But for now, you're sad. And that's okay. Rather than feel bad about feeling sad, just feel sad. Going through the emotions is the fastest way to heal your grief. So go ahead and feel sad. Think and write and express and ponder. Keep up with your daily responsibilities as best you can, postponing what can wait, taking time to do what must be done now.

Journaling Suggestions

Describe your sadness. One way to do this is to choose three letters of the alphabet and three or more words that begin with each. Feel free to use another piece of paper.

Sample   Your description

D: dark, depressing,
     discouraging

E: empty, excruciating,
     endless, exhausting

F: a fierce fight that fatigues

Illustrate your sadness. You may use pictures or words. What does your sadness look like? Feel like? Act like? How does it move? Change? Fill this space with your sadness.

Some people write poems or songs about the person or event that caused their sadness. Others write stories or draw images. What do you want people to know about the person you care about or the event that has occurred? What feelings and thoughts are roaming in your mind and heart? Write them here (continue on extra sheets of paper).

Share Your Sadness with God

When Jesus cried, onlookers recognized it as an expression of love (John 11:35–36). God understands and feels sadness. He wants to help you express your sadness in honest and healing ways. The Bible contains many sad experiences. In fact, an entire book of the Bible is poems expressing grief. In this book, called Lamentations, the writer mourned the capture of Jerusalem. This takeover of the Israelites' homeland brought captivity, starvation, slavery, and worse. Joy came gradually, not instantly, and the writer took time to fully grieve for the tragedy.

Read the following sample from Lamentations.

> *He has broken my teeth with gravel;*
> *he has trampled me in the dust.*
> *I have been deprived of peace;*
> *I have forgotten what prosperity is.*
> *So I say, "My splendor is gone*
> *and all that I had hoped from the* LORD.*"*

> *I remember my affliction and my wandering,*
> *the bitterness and the gall.*
> *I well remember them,*
> *and my soul is downcast within me.*
> *Yet this I call to mind*
> *and therefore I have hope:*

> *Because of the* LORD'S *great love we are not consumed,*
> *for his compassions never fail.*
> *They are new every morning;*
> *great is your faithfulness.*
> *I say to myself, "The* LORD *is my portion;*
> *therefore I will wait for him."*

> *The* LORD *is good to those whose hope is in him,*
> *to the one who seeks him.*
> *Lamentations 3:16–25*

Journaling Suggestions

Write your own passage of sorrow. Pour out your feelings before God.

Hold, Hide, and Heal

God refuses to let sadness have the last word. Three actions are central to making it through the sadness and recognizing the good that God continues to send into your life. Jot or doodle your responses to each in the white spaces.

HOLD

Find family members and friends who will hold you. Holding includes physical actions like hugs, emotional actions like standing by you, and spiritual actions like holding you before God's throne in prayer. Touch, tenderness, and prayer are like balm on a sore wound. Caring family members and friends fill in some of the gaps your dead loved one (or the sad event) leaves behind. Illustrate ways you've been held. Then illustrate and cross out types of holding that might *bring* pain rather than heal it.

HIDE

Death, the diagnosis of a serious illness, and other life-shaking experiences require recovery time. You may not be able to keep up your usual pace. You'll probably need at least a weekend to recover from the initial shock, and you'll need more bits of time later. You may simply need an afternoon to sleep or sit. Take time to hide and recuperate—then return to activity. Refuse to let your hiding habit become a permanent one. What is your favorite way to hide? (Examples: reading, sleeping, thinking, listening to music, staying home. See chapter 5 for more retreat/hiding ideas.)

HEAL

Death or other tragedy inflicts wounds as real as any physical injury. You need healing time. You'll go through stages of pain similar to those of a physical injury. To the left of each phase of physical healing write how your emotional healing might be like it.

numbness
excruciating pain
dull, aching pain
itching
scab
scar
returned use of injured part

Some injuries heal on their own. Others need help from a doctor or medicine. What help might you need to heal fully from your injury?

Embrace Hope

Another H word that is crucial to moving through sadness is HOPE. Hope makes holding, hiding, and healing effective, because it knows there will be joy on the other side. Hope is the difference between giving up and going on. Even a glimmer of hope helps Melanie refuse to consider suicide or other acts of desperation.

There is hope in heaven because there will be no more sorrow, crying, or pain.

And God shall wipe away all tears from their eyes; and there shall be no more death, neither sorrow, nor crying, neither shall there be any more pain: for the former things are passed away.
Revelation 21:4 KJV

There is also hope on earth. Recall Lamentations 3:22–23:

Because of the LORD's great love we are not consumed, for his compassions never fail. They are new every morning; great is your faithfulness.

God will take care of us. We'll notice little pinpricks and glimmers of happiness even during the deepest sadness.

Journaling Suggestions

Why is hope so powerful? Draw, describe, or define hope.

Name or draw the reasons you feel hopeless right now or have felt hopeless in the past.

How does God's love bring hope to your hopelessness?

Not all hope works; some hope is just whistling in the dark. But hope in God works because it is true hope. It's not just wishful thinking. God is real, God is consistent, God is powerful. Because of this, we can trust him. Examine these Bible verses about God's hope. How does each impact you personally? What other Bible promises might you add to this list?

Bible promise	What I like about it

I am confident of this, that the one [God] who began a good work among you will bring it to completion by the day of Jesus Christ (Philippians 1:6 NRSV).

Do not let your hearts be troubled. Trust in God; trust also in me. In my Father's house are many rooms; if it were not so, I would have told you . . . And if I go and prepare a place for you, I will come back and take you to be with me that you also may be where I am (John 14:1–3).

Brothers, we do not want you to be ignorant about those who fall asleep, or to grieve like the rest of men, who have no hope. We believe that Jesus died and rose again and so we

36

*believe that God will bring
with Jesus those who have
fallen asleep in him . . . After
that, we . . . will be caught up
with them in the clouds to
meet the Lord in the air. And
so we will be with the Lord
forever (1 Thessalonians
4:13–14, 17).*

*For we do not have a high
priest who is unable to sympathize with our weaknesses,
but we have one who has
been tempted in every way,
just as we are—yet was without sin. Let us then approach
the throne of grace with confidence, so that we may receive
mercy and find grace to help
us in our time of need
(Hebrews 4:15–16).*

How does God's personal love give you hope? How does he make it possible to have hope in the middle of despair? To get through your darkest moments?

Live On with Security

As Melanie grieved and healed, she also moved on with life. Nobody ever replaced her grandfather, but God gave Melanie other people to love her. Her friend Bill listened to Melanie and loved her as she was. Several years later Melanie's mother-in-law gave her the parenting love and wise advice her grandfather had given. Melanie began to see God as the ultimate provider of her needs. He cared for her through people—one-of-a-kind, irreplaceable, precious people. None took the place of another, and each was missed when he or she moved out of her life. But all wove together to form the tapestry of God's care. That beauty and hope sustained Melanie as she walked on through her sadness.

CHAPTER 3

How Could I Do Something So Stupid?

FIND FORGIVENESS FROM GUILT AND RELEASE FROM REGRET

I wish I hadn't lost my temper. Ted had been acting like a real jerk since I started dating other guys. I got fed up with it and told him to go away and leave me alone. Then he had that terrible wreck. I feel like it's all my fault," said Jennifer.

"Why did I take that dare?" lamented Ted. "I should have known better than to race down that narrow road. It was just that one curve I couldn't get around. But when the van flipped over, Rand was killed and Kelly was paralyzed. She'll be in the hospital for months and will never walk or run again. She was counting on a soccer scholarship to pay for college."

"Why did Ted drive so wildly? And why didn't I put my seat belt on?" fretted Kelly. "I still might have been hurt when Ted's van flipped over, but not nearly as badly. I'd still have use of my legs and I could still play soccer. I'd even give up the soccer if I could walk again."

"I wish I'd spent last Saturday with Kelly as I'd planned," said Hannah. " I stayed home to study. Now Kelly and I will never get to take that mountain hike. She'll be in the hospital for at least six months and then in a wheelchair for life."

Following closely on the heals of sadness come feelings of guilt. Jennifer, Ted, Kelly, and Hannah feel guilty about the auto accident. They feel guilty about what they did and guilty about what they didn't do. Even though nothing can change what happened, they can't help thinking about ways they could have prevented it.

This regret is part of working through guilt and grief. It's okay, even good, to feel bad about what you did wrong or mistakenly in the past. It not only helps you heal, it also prevents you from hurting other people in the future.

Journaling Suggestions

What do you regret most about the sad thing that has happened to you?

If you could relive the experience or turn back the clock, what would you do differently? The same?

Draw a cartoon strip (stick figures or words only are fine) to show how you wish things had gone.

Is there any word or action in your cartoon that you actually can redo? For example, Kelly can't climb a mountain, but Hannah and she could go to another scenic spot. Describe or doodle that action here.

Read on to discover what to do about actions you cannot redo or change.

Avoid the Extremes

There are two very dangerous extremes for dealing with guilt and regret.

The first is to ignore or minimize it, to decide that since we can't help making mistakes, we just have to live with them.

The second is to feel so bad about the past that we refuse to go on, refuse to enjoy life again, refuse to forgive ourselves or the one who hurt us.

The best path is to balance regret with going on; to ask forgiveness from God and the people we harmed; to make changes related to that forgiveness; to mourn over the wrong; to redeem the past as best we can; and to keep from making future mistakes.

Journaling Suggestions

Doodle or describe a time you tried to ignore or minimize a sin, mistake, or destructive choice.

Doodle or describe a time you refused to forgive, refused to go on, or stayed in the past.

Doodle or draw a circumstance you feel guilty about and want to change. What forgiveness will you ask? What changes do you think God wants you to make related to your forgiveness?

Find Forgiveness for Guilt

Our actions matter. It wasn't wrong for Jennifer to tell Ted to leave her alone. It was wrong for her to explode in anger. Jennifer's anger stirred Ted's anger. Ted chose to drive wildly rather than channel his angry pain down a safe path. Ted never meant to hurt anyone, but his choices led to Rand's death and Kelly's paralysis. He can say "I'm sorry," but that won't erase what has happened. What now?

They can use 1 John 1:8–9 as a guide, divided here for emphasis:

If we claim to be without sin, we deceive ourselves and the truth is not in us.

It is silly to say we haven't done wrong if we have. Declaring that it was not our fault won't change the facts. Conversely, acting like the scum of the earth who is totally responsible for every wrong and who can never show her face again won't help either. So we must first admit what we did, realize that all our actions impact others in some way, and decide what to do next.

If we confess our sins,

Jesus calls this admission process confession—we tell God what we did and our feelings about it. We may have done wrong or we may have failed to do right. Often God will urge us to tell a fellow Christian or

44

confess to the one we have wronged. When we tell God, he promises that . . .

he is faithful and just

He will continue to love us no matter what. We don't have to worry about losing God's love.

and will forgive us our sins

He will not only keep loving us, he will forgive us and love us just like we'd never done wrong.

and purify us from all unrighteousness.

And best of all, after God forgives us, he will change us: He'll replace the bad action or attitude with rightness, goodness, and love. Of course we'll need to *agree* to these changes— he never forces himself on us. He might guide us to make restitution for harm caused, change a dangerous habit, or develop a more loving one. This takes time and repetition, but it will happen eventually and certainly.

45

Walk through the confession and cleansing process yourself, noticing your sins, confessing them to God, and talking with him about the changes he'd like to make in you. Ted might say:

If we claim to be without sin, we deceive ourselves and the truth is not in us.

What I do matters. In this case I have hurt Kelly and her family. I have killed Rand and hurt his family. I didn't mean to, but my irresponsible behavior brought all of them tremendous pain.

If we confess our sins,

I confess that I have used my anger as an excuse for driving wildly. I confess that my wild driving caused Rand's death and Kelly's paralysis. I confess that I was more concerned about my pride than my friends' safety.

he is faithful and just

Thank you for loving me anyway, God. I don't know how you do it. I deserve worse than what Rand and Kelly got.

and will forgive us our sins

Thank you for forgiving me. How can I forgive myself? I'll need your help.

and purify us from all unrighteousness.

With your power I'll tame my temper. I'll drive like the lives of those in my car depend on me. I'll help Kelly stay caught up in school and do whatever else she needs. I'll ask forgiveness from her, her parents, and Rand's parents.

46

Journaling Suggestions

Fill in what you'd say:

If we claim to be without sin, we deceive ourselves and the

truth is not in us.

If we confess our sins,

he is faithful and just

and will forgive us our sins

> and purify us from all unrighteousness.

Though God forgives instantly and purifies day by day, Satan will remind you of your past and try to convince you that you are wretched and worthless. Deliberately turn away from his lies and turn to people who help you live the truth. Review your sin every time you think about it, reminding yourself that God has forgiven you and you can change your present and future.

The solution to your guilt is threefold:

1. Request and receive God's forgiveness and cleansing.
2. Ask forgiveness of people who have been harmed by your action.
3. Choose to do right from here on. Refuse to let the past doom your future.

Journaling Suggestions

You talked with God in the previous journaling section. Now write a letter to the person you most want forgiveness from, even if that person is dead or will never see this letter.

Perhaps hardest of all is to forgive yourself. Talk with yourself about why it is hard to forgive yourself, why you are worth forgiving, and the changes you will make to live your forgiveness.

Dear Me,

Love, Me

Release Regrets

Some past actions are not sins at all. Kelly's and Hannah's choices impacted the accident but did not cause it. Kelly refused to value her life when she rode without her seat belt. It may not have been sin, but it was certainly dangerous. If it was sin, it was sin against herself.

Hannah's decision to study instead of mountain climb was a good decision—she needed to do well on her exam. Her action was neither sinful nor destructive, but she feels bad that she'll never get the mountain climbing experience back. She also may feel that if Kelly had been on the mountain with her, she wouldn't have been riding in Ted's car. Hannah must rename her actions as regret, not guilt. Then she must think through her regrets until she is comfortable with their memory.

Notice the nature of your choices to help you know how to respond to them. Were you responsible for the pain, or do you simply regret not having more time with your friend? Did you contribute to the problem, though you didn't directly cause it? Did you sin, or do you just wish things had been different? Sin can only heal after forgiveness from God, from yourself, and often from the person you hurt. Regret heals after being walked through, relived, talked about, and sometimes shared. Both sin and regret need attention, time, and healing.

Another action you may need to rename is false guilt. Kelly feels the accident was her fault because she had been lax about church attendance and daily Bible study. She thinks God was jolting her from her complacency. But God is not a "wait-to-catch-you-doing-wrong-and-then-get-you" kind of God. Fast driving, not spiritual neglect, caused the accident.

❖ One sin I did that I wish I hadn't:

❖ One thing I regret about the sad thing that happened:

❖ One false guilt I carry:

What if you can't tell which is which? What if you think it's regret, but it may be sin? What if you think it's true guilt, but it may be false guilt? Worry less about naming the action than about healing it. Sin and regret, true guilt and false guilt require review, rethinking, and deciding what to do next. It won't hurt to ask forgiveness even if it was not sin. Ask God to help you take the actions he wants you to take.

REVIEW

As you did at the beginning of this chapter, remember what happened, how you wish it had been different, and how you feel about it. Find genuine forgiveness for genuine wrong, and true freedom from regret or imagined guilt. Invite God to review with you. In the left column draw, doodle, or express in poetry your review.

RETHINK

Feeling forgiven or recovering from regret seldom happens in one review. Though God forgives instantly, people aren't so quick about it. And we may have trouble forgiving ourselves. Kelly went through a time when she didn't even want to see Ted, let alone forgive him. Take the time you need to give and accept forgiveness, to find peace with your past, to free yourself from regret. Just keep rethinking and praying. Healing will come. Jot or doodle some of your "re-thoughts" and "reprayers" in the left column.

DECIDE WHAT'S NEXT

What now? What do you think God wants you to do about the past actions you can't redo? Hannah told Kelly that she regretted not taking one last mountain climb. She and Kelly planned a different type of trip. Like Hannah and Kelly, you can refuse to let the past doom your future. The following are sample "what's nexts." Choose the ones that apply to your situation and personalize them.

❖ *Ask forgiveness.* Ted asked forgiveness from Kelly. I will ask forgiveness from _____.
The words I will use are:

❖ *Give forgiveness.* Kelly chose to forgive Ted. It wasn't easy, nor did she feel much like she had forgiven him at first. She let the forgiveness be a gradual process rather than trying to forgive and forget instantly. I will forgive _____ for _____ .
The words I will use are:

```
┌─────────────────────────────────────────┐
│                                           │
│                                           │
│                                           │
│                                           │
│                                           │
│                                           │
└─────────────────────────────────────────┘
```

❖ *Show new care.* Ted cannot give Kelly the use of her legs. But he can get her homework while she's in the hospital. I'll show new care by:

```
┌─────────────────────────────────────────┐
│                                           │
│                                           │
│                                           │
│                                           │
│                                           │
│                                           │
└─────────────────────────────────────────┘
```

55

❖ *Make restitution.* The van Ted damaged belonged to his family. He paid for the repairs by putting a part of each paycheck toward the bill. I'll make restitution for _____ by:

```
┌─────────────────────────────────────────┐
│                                           │
│                                           │
│                                           │
│                                           │
│                                           │
│                                           │
└─────────────────────────────────────────┘
```

❖ *Say good-bye to the one who has died.* Jennifer, Ted, Kelly, and Hannah found their own ways of saying good-bye to Rand. Jennifer wrote him a letter. Ted told his parents how much Rand had meant to him. Kelly sat by Rand's grave and told God all the things she wanted to tell Rand. Hannah wrote a poem that she later set to music. I'll say good-bye to _____ by:

```
┌─────────────────────────────────────────┐
│                                         │
│                                         │
│                                         │
│                                         │
│                                         │
│                                         │
└─────────────────────────────────────────┘
```

❖ *Live the good taught by the one who died.* Kelly had been impressed by Rand's upbeat attitude. He saw possibilities for good in the darkest circumstances. As Kelly fought to recover from her injuries and to manipulate her wheelchair, she developed an attitude like his. _____ taught me to _____. I'll do this by:

```
┌─────────────────────────────────────────┐
│                                         │
│                                         │
│                                         │
│                                         │
│                                         │
└─────────────────────────────────────────┘
```

❖ *Adjust to my unchangeable condition.* Kelly cannot change her paralysis, so she must figure out ways to get from place to place. While keeping her ears open for medical breakthroughs, she has learned to maneuver her wheelchair with dexterity. She vows to become as mobile as anyone with working legs. She must also find another way to pay for college. I will adjust to _____ by:

```
┌─────────────────────────────────────┐
│                                       │
│                                       │
│                                       │
│                                       │
│                                       │
└─────────────────────────────────────┘
```

❖ *Keep from repeating the same mistake.* Ted determined to refuse dares no matter how strongly friends taunted him. He also decided to get his anger under control before getting behind the wheel. I'll keep from repeating _____ by:

```
┌─────────────────────────────────────┐
│                                       │
│                                       │
│                                       │
│                                       │
│                                       │
└─────────────────────────────────────┘
```

❖ *Grow a different kind of good.* Hannah and Kelly can't go on trips until Kelly gets out of the hospital. In the meantime they can travel up and down the hospital halls, spend hours talking, take silly photographs of each other. I'll acquire a different kind of good by:

```
┌─────────────────────────────────────┐
│                                       │
│                                       │
│                                       │
│                                       │
│                                       │
└─────────────────────────────────────┘
```

❖ *Talk about it honestly.* Rand's brother was very upset with Ted. When Ted asked him for forgiveness, he didn't say, "That's okay." He openly said, "I'm very angry with you. I know I'll be able to forgive you eventually and I'm trying now, but you need to give me a little time and space." I need to talk to or listen to _____ about:

```



```

❖ *Share the blame.* In a sense everybody's responsible but nobody's totally responsible. Jennifer spoke cruelly. The boys in the other van made a dare. Ted took the dare. Rand and Kelly wore no seat belts. Each person must choose to accept his or her part of the blame, to grieve about that, and to make better choices in the future. Ted said, "Jennifer made me angry. But I didn't have to let my anger cloud my actions. That was really stupid." I'll share the blame for _____ by:

```



```

❖ *Redeem the past.* Do all you can to bring good out of the rubble. The sad choice or event can never be erased, but the sadness can motivate us to create good. For example, Jennifer deliberately talks out her

58

differences calmly rather than igniting fury. She cannot help the way people react to her, but she can create circumstances that promote calmness, such as choosing a private time, explaining rather than attacking, taking her part of the blame, being consistent, refusing to use people, being kind with her honesty. I'll redeem my past by:

┌───┐
│   │
│   │
│   │
│   │
└───┘

❖ *Surround yourself with people who care.* Some fellow Christians will be helpful in your struggle with guilt and forgiveness. Others will want you to feel instantly better or to suffer forever. Find friends and family members who encourage you to receive and live forgiveness, who listen as you learn to accept God's forgiveness and forgive yourself. Name people who have done this or could do this for you:

┌───┐
│   │
│   │
│   │
│   │
└───┘

Commit to Future Excellence

The worst sin or mistake is one you don't learn from, one that changes nothing about you or your relationships. It's nearly impossible to make all your choices correct ones. But with attention you can make more of them right. When you depend on God's strength and obey his Word, you can keep from repeating past mistakes. You can prevent pain and cultivate joy. You can change the world by the way you live in it. Choose to create good.

> *I have set before you life and death, blessings and curses. Now choose life, so that you and your children may live and that you may love the LORD your God, listen to his voice, and hold fast to him. For the LORD is your life.*
> Deuteronomy 30:19–20

You can choose to value people: "I'll express my anger calmly but firmly." "I'll use kind words rather than cutting ones." "I'll point out the good rather than harp on the bad." "I'll refuse to be a user."

A way I'll value people is:_____

_____

You can choose to value life: "I'll drive as though everyone's life depends on me." "I'll insist that everyone in my car wear seat belts." "I'll refuse to drive if I've drunk alcohol or when I'm not concentrating on my driving." "I'll turn down dares and other stupid tricks because someone could get hurt—permanently."

A way I'll value life is:_____

_____

You can choose to value happiness: "My words and actions will make people's day, not destroy it." "I'll soothe arguments rather than escalate them." "I'll include everyone in activities." "I'll listen when others share something important."

A way I'll value happiness is:_____

_____

You can choose to value the present and the future: "I'll make sure I take some time for study and some time for people." "I'll tell people what I like about them today, knowing that none of us has a guarantee of tomorrow."

A way I'll value the present and the future is:_____

_____

CHAPTER 4

I'm So Mad I Can't See Straight

MOVE THROUGH YOUR ANGER

My aunt was the picture of health," explained Helena. "She ate well, took good care of herself, exercised, and did all the things you're supposed to do to live a long life. She was also in great shape spiritually and emotionally. She taught Sunday school for thirty years and made everybody around her feel important. She and my uncle had the most fun-loving marriage I've ever seen. They were wonderfully happy. I loved being around them. We spent at least one weekend a month together. The way my aunt lived her faith and cared about people made me certain that God is real and that he cares.

"Last month she went in for minor surgery, reacted to the anesthesia, and died. Besides missing her, I'm just plain mad. It's not fair that such a wonderful person died so young. Why not my other aunt who's testy and doesn't even like people? Why not a bedridden person living in a nursing home who would welcome death? Why does anesthesia work safely on most people but not my aunt? She was only fifty. She should have had at least twenty more years. It's just not right. I need my aunt and I miss her."

Some things in life just aren't fair. The people who hate life live on; the people who love life die early. It makes us really mad. And so it should. Accidents, disease, and disabilities are distortions of God's good world. They are insults to God. Anger is the sadness that says, "I hate this! It's not right!"

Accidents and death are testimony to the imperfection of this world, the need for a better place. Death makes us sad. It makes God sad too. Death is a result of sin, not a part of God's original plan. He weeps right along with us when someone we care about dies or gets hurt. Then he provides the better place, a place called heaven where things are perfect, a place Helena's aunt can enjoy now and where Helena can look forward to joining her.

When things go badly, some people automatically blame God. They see him as:

CONTROLLING *unfeeling* Vengeful Selfish

someone who punishes without explanation   out to get them

Uncommunicative   **disconnected**

impersonal   UNINVOLVED

64

I'd get mad at God too if I thought he was like this. Thankfully, he's not. We've got to see God as he really is, not as we think he is or as someone else tells us he is. Search the Scripture and get to know God personally. There we discover God as a caring parent who hurts along with his children (Psalm 63:9). We see a God who provides good gifts (James 1:16–17) and not bad ones (Job 1:22; 42:7). He's not the cause of bad things; he's the source for getting through them.

Circle the characteristics you see in God when things go wrong. Add some of your own in the spaces provided.

caring _____ *sympathetic* **STRONG**

stable   LOVING   Source of Light

_____ **UNDERSTANDING** _____

See Things Clearly

Healing your anger begins by seeing it clearly. When you're mad, it's nearly impossible to see straight. So you must deliberately set your eyes on the truth and determine to see things the way they really are. Examine each scene and respond to it. The first scene in our clearing view is perhaps the most important one:

Scene 1: God Is on Your Side

God is not the cause of your pain; he's the healer of it. Adjust your vision to see God as he is, a caring God who wants to walk beside you through the rage, who has the power to heal your pain, and who can deliver the certainty of eternal security. Take his hand and walk on through the anger, confident that you will come out whole on the other side. He will take care of you.

> *I lift up my eyes to the hills—*
> *where does my help come from?*
> *My help comes from the* LORD,
> *the Maker of heaven and earth . . .*
> *indeed, he who watches over Israel*
> *will neither slumber nor sleep . . .*
> *the* LORD *will watch over your coming and going*
> *both now and forevermore.*
>
> *Psalm 121:1–2, 4, 8*

65

Talk with God about his presence and care related to the current sad thing in your life. What do you say to God? What does he say back? Use the word bubbles on the next page to frame your conversation.

Scene 2: Anger Is Not a Sin

Anger is an important emotion given to us by our caring God. It's a warning sign that something is wrong. You've

got to find what it is so you can fix it. Perhaps that some-thing is pain within you, pain in someone you know, or an injustice that needs righting. Anger serves good purposes when managed correctly. In fact, the Bible encourages us to be angry when the time is right. Anger becomes sin only when expressed in destructive ways. These two translations of Ephesians 4:26a (KJV and NIV) make clear both the impor-tance of anger and the need to pay attention to how we express it.

Be ye angry, and sin not.   *In your anger do not sin.*

We can go ahead and be   But we can't hurt people
angry.   by the way we express it.

Anger is a sensitive animal. It must be handled deliber-ately and carefully or it will attack us and those around us. It must neither be ignored nor let out unharnessed. Draw the animal or combination of animals your current anger resembles. You can use the face from one animal, the feet from another, and so on. Feel free to add parts from a totally fictitious animal.

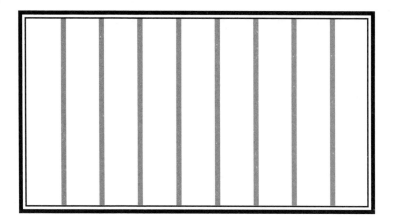

Scene 3: Anger Is a Symptom of Pain

Anger seldom stands alone. It usually means pain lying below the surface. It can mean sadness or loneliness or hurt. God cares not only about your anger, but about the sad events that feed it. He knows Helena wouldn't be mad if her aunt hadn't died and she didn't miss her so deeply. God values Helena's love for her aunt and weeps along with her. He wants to heal the pain behind the anger. He wants Helena and you to tell him about your anger, to let him understand you, love you, and heal you.

Begin to resolve your anger by recognizing the pain behind it. Accept anger as a form of grief, an expression of pain, a type of sadness. Draw or describe a time you've been:

*   mad because you're sad ("I just can't believe she's really dead.")

* mad because you're lonely ("He's the only one who understood me.")

* mad because of an injustice—perhaps someone innocent suffered at the hand of someone guilty ("He shouldn't get away with this!")

* mad because trouble doesn't seem to be happening to anyone else ("Why my aunt? Nobody else has this problem!")

* mad for a reason you can't figure out ("I'm so furious I could explode!")

Put Anger Where It Belongs

Even when you know God is on your side, you may still find yourself mad at him. That's okay. God can handle it. If you're mad at God, tell him so and tell him why. He understands the sadness and pain behind your anger. He can help you understand it. He is eager to heal you. He'll show you what to do about your anger. Let him help you walk through the anger to the peace on the other side.

Then refuse to stay mad at God, mainly because God didn't do it (see chapter 6 for more on why bad things happen). Go ahead and put your anger where it belongs. Be mad at whatever or whoever really caused the problem. Circle or add the cause of your angry pain.

an accident   an infection   a drunk driver   a tornado

an uncaring friend   a thoughtless teacher or leader

a selfish person   a disability   a stupid mistake

a tumor or other cancer   a cruel person

a toxic dumper   _____

69

Seeing who or what caused the anger is more than just placing blame. It's locating a cause, noticing why it hurts us, finding ways to forgive if forgiveness is needed, and moving through the hurt to the healing on the other side. Helena is mad at the accident that occurred on the operating table. The anesthesiologist didn't realize Helena's aunt would react fatally. No one's sure if he was negligent or if it was pure accident.

Think It Through

Once you've located the source of your anger, talk with God about why this person, event, circumstance, or action bothers you so much. Deliberately think it through, feel it deeply, and discover what God wants you to do about it. Mentally go through what you feel like doing, and then cross out what not to do. Ask God to guide you to his solution for the dilemma.

Like all grief, anger takes time to heal, and it may return several times before it leaves for good. If the event were a small one like being snubbed at the lunch table, an hour of after-school fuming may take care of the pain. Helena's anger over her aunt's accidental death, and Kelly's anger at Ted for the car crash that paralyzed her, will take much longer to resolve. Kelly's anger resurfaces every time she sees a soccer game. Each time the anger comes, she walks on through it with God at her side:

> *God, I can feel it coming again. Why did Ted have to take that stupid dare? His pride cost me my legs. I'd so love to be out there running again. I'd much rather walk down the aisle during graduation than roll in this chair. I don't know how I'm ever going to pay for college now. I'm hurting, God. I want Ted to have the paralyzed legs, not me. Even as I say that I know he feels bad, that he regrets it as much as I do. But still I lash out at him. Heal me from that, God. Please help me think through my actions before I do something equally destructive to someone I care about. Paralyzed legs are the pits, God. I can hardly wait to have new legs in heaven, but I'm not ready to die quite yet. I wish I could have my new legs now. Gosh I'm mad. Please help me do the best I can with this broken body. Thanks for your power.*

Kelly moves toward peace as she talks things over with God. This process may take a single conversation or many agonizing days. Take whatever time you need, maintaining that precarious balance between ignoring your anger and letting anger lead to sin. Let God guide you through the minefield, past the explosions, and to the peace that passes understanding.

Journaling Suggestions

Write your prayer of present or past anger, being absolutely honest with God. Don't worry about spelling or grammar—just pour it out.

Psalm 4:4, from which Ephesians 4:26 is quoted, suggests silence as a tool for managing anger:

In your anger do not sin; when you are on your beds, search your hearts and be silent.

Notice how silence is different from holding anger in.

✻ Silence is an inward and active searching that heals.
   ✻ It keeps you from attacking people with your anger.
      ✻ It keeps you from saying something you'll later regret.
         ✻ It gives you time to talk with God about what to do with your anger.
            ✻ It takes anger seriously without letting it hurt people or things;
               ✻ So rather than a destroyer, your anger becomes a healer.

Journaling Suggestions

Now draw or write how silence helps you with anger.

Adjust the Vent

As waves of anger roll over Helena, she first fumes against the anesthesiologist, then against the doctor who recommended the surgery, then against the anesthesia drug. She trembles with exhaustion following every wave of anger, but each wave comes with a little less intensity.

This intensity is exactly what gives anger a bad name. Helena's anger is so strong that it wears her out. When her friend Richard gets mad, he wants to wear somebody else out. When he thinks about his alcoholic father, he feels like putting his fists through a wall, and too often he does.

Anger is such a volatile emotion that it must be carefully harnessed. Our goal is to let anger heal not harm, to get anger to decrease in intensity with each prayer or expression. Helena has discovered how to do this. But each time Richard ponders his anger, he gets angrier. Because his anger is so explosive, he tries not to think about it at all.

The problem with Richard's approach is that anger always finds a way out. Unharnessed, anger comes out as vengefulness, sarcasm, violence, and abuse. Held in, it transforms into depression, cold treatment, moodiness, and irritability. Both scenarios set Richard up for behavior he regrets. This leads to guilt and more anger—a frustrating and vicious cycle Richard wants to break. Like a pressure cooker, anger has got to be vented a bit at a time; if we open it all at once, it explodes.

Richard has to open his anger valve long enough to let off the steam. Then he can open his anger all the way up to think and pray it through. Like many of us, Richard uses physical activity to vent the intensity of his anger. It's amazing how far he can drive a golf ball when he's mad at it. Avoid competitive play, driving, or any other activity that puts others in the range of your anger. Choose private sports, physical work, and other energy absorbers as you think and pray through your anger.

Letitia has the opposite problem. She also holds her anger in, but for a different reason. She thinks anger is wrong and is simply an attitude problem. Because she feels guilty about anger, she refuses to get mad at all. Her anger eats at her from within, chiseling away her confidence and her joy. She fights a low-grade sadness she never can figure out—it's anger converted to depression. She must adjust her vent the other way. She must give herself permission to feel more angry.

Decide What to Do about Your Anger

As you think about, pray about, and vent your anger, invite God to show you what he wants you to do about it. Sometimes praying, thinking, talking, and feeling are enough. Other times a human helper and more actions are needed. Proceed carefully and follow God's guidance as he shows you how to "be . . . angry and sin not" (Ephesians 4:26).

Journaling Suggestions

When your anger needs more than mental action, feel free to give it a little venting. What keeps your anger from becoming a destroyer?

* _Paint_: Depict exactly how you feel. Let color and texture express your rage.

* _Create_: Write a song, draw a picture.

✻ <u>Walk</u>: Take a long walk privately or with a friend. Walk as fast as your anger feels.

✻ <u>Write</u>: Record all the words and actions you feel like doing, even those you would never do.

✻ <u>Talk</u>: Find a friend or family member who will listen while the angry words tumble out.

✻ <u>Touch</u>: Enjoy a hug from someone who genuinely cares while your angry tears flow.

✻ <u>Sports</u>: Choose private anger absorbers like running, working out, bench pressing, aerobics, and basketball.

✻ <u>Work</u>: Attack a messy closet, chop firewood, mow the lawn, repair your car, or clear the blockage from the creek.

✻ <u>Other</u>:

Which way do you need to vent your anger? Do you need to let it out a little more gradually or a little more forcefully? Avoiding the extremes, mark the place you are right now. Then draw an arrow from that spot to where you want to move.

Explain why. Feel free to add your own vent descriptions.

hold it all in	tell someone I'm angry and why	exercise off the excess	let it all out unharnessed

You don't have to be afraid to walk through anger. God will guide you safely through it. Adjust your vent to enable you to feel the anger, agonize over it, and let it out in ways that heal rather than hurt.

Explore the following possibilities, talking with God about which actions would work best to heal your particular situation. Notice how anger management fits into the whole pattern of Christian behavior.

This first set of anger-healing attitudes and actions comes from Ephesians 4:25–32. Check the ones that would work best for you. Then write words and actions with which you might do each.

<u>Put off falsehood and speak truthfully to [your] neighbor.</u> Rather than blame someone else, Ted decided to admit that he stupidly took the dare. I'll . . .

<u>[Be] members of one body.</u> Helena found herself taking her anger out on her brother. But she realized he was also upset about their aunt's death, and she began to treat him kindly. I'll . . .

<u>Do not let the sun go down while you are still angry.</u> Kelly's brother had trouble doing this, so he vowed to talk about his

anger as calmly as possible. He knew it wouldn't do any good to hold it in. I'll . . .

Do not give the devil a foothold. Helena felt like revenge, but she knew this wouldn't solve anything. She decided to talk directly and kindly to the physicians about what happened.

He who has been stealing [or doing any kind of wrong] must steal no longer, but must work, doing something useful with his own hands, that he may have something to share with those in need. Helena decided to transform some of her anger into making people feel welcome like her aunt did. Actively caring for others helped. I'll . . .

<u>Do not let any unwholesome talk come out of your mouths.</u> Helena vowed not to gossip about the hospital or the physician; she has also kept up her resolve to talk kindly to her brother. I'll . . .

<u>[Say] only what is helpful for building others up according to their needs, that it may benefit those who listen.</u> When she talks about anger, Helena concentrates on making things better, not on getting back at someone. I'll . . .

<u>Do not grieve the Holy Spirit of God.</u> Kelly knows that hostile feelings about her paralysis won't help her or God. She resolves to find a way to enjoy life anyway and heal from the anger. I'll . . .

<u>Get rid of all bitterness, rage and anger.</u> Helena can't stop the bitter feelings from starting, but she can keep them from staying by thinking them through until she feels better. I'll . . .

<u>[Get rid of] brawling and slander, along with every form of malice.</u> Richard stops these because they only make him or someone else madder. I'll . . .

<u>Be kind and compassionate to one another.</u> Kelly remembers that Ted feels terrible about what he did. I'll . . .

<u>Forgive each other, just as in Christ God forgave you.</u> If Helena doesn't forgive, the anger will live on. So she forgives the doctors even when she doesn't feel like it and keeps on forgiving until she feels like she really means it. Forgiveness comes gradually, not instantly. I'll . . .

You've examined guidelines and attitudes that lead to anger-reducing actions. Below are specific actions based on these guidelines and attitudes. Which do you think God wants you to take? Write or draw next to each how it would help your angry situation.

Talk directly to the one you're angry with. It takes a big person to express anger in a caring way. Be this kind of person. It also takes a big person to hear anger and not lash back. Even if you express your anger kindly, the other person might get angrier and take it out on you. Or the talk may bring you closer.

Mentally compose a conversation with the person or thing you're angry with. It may be a friend, a politician, a disease, a disability, a hurricane, or a circumstance. Helena's mad at the anesthesia. Just thinking it through can disperse the anger and cleanse your pain.

81

Write a letter to the one you're angry with. Keep it at least two weeks before deciding whether to mail it. If your letter is harmful in any way, don't mail it. Tear it up. If the source of your anger is dead, or is a germ or a circumstance, pretend to deliver the letter.

Turn your anger into something positive. For example, rather than rage at cancer, study to become a researcher who will wipe it out forever. Rather than complain about the medical professionals who botched the surgery, write a letter of appreciation to doctors who did care.

When you don't feel a direct conversation or letter is best, let an empty chair or an understanding friend play the person or circumstance you're angry with. Tell this stand-in exactly what you think of him, why you're angry, and what you wish he would do.

82

Let a pillow, piece of paper, or other object become the situation you're angry at. Hit or dismantle that object bit by bit as you tell it why you're mad. Helena can't attack an accident, but she can tear a picture of it to tiny shreds. She's then emotionally ready to look forward to reunion with her aunt in heaven.

Through conversation or letter, forgive the person you're angry with. Forgiveness is tough—you'll need to draw on

God's power to do it. Two tips can help: 1. "Forget" doesn't have to accompany "forgive." 2. You don't have to feel ready to forgive before you do it. You can say the words and think the thoughts until your feelings agree.

Three ideas don't work in any angry circumstance. Describe why these won't work in your case:

It never helps to take anger out on someone else. Some people kick their dog. Others yell at their mom or little brother. The fancy word for this is abuse.

83

Abuse won't heal my anger because . . .

It never helps to take it out on yourself. The extreme example of this is suicide, but many varieties of self-destructive behavior exist. Examples include: self-criticism, blaming yourself even after you've been forgiven, believing you're a worm, over-eating, taking drugs (a slow suicide), drinking alcohol.

Taking my anger out on myself won't work because . . .

It never helps to ignore anger. It either becomes depression (frequently a depression you can't quite figure out), or it explodes into attack mode. One little thing sets off a flood of everything you've been angry about for months or years. You may simply yell, or you may attack a shopping mall full of people with a gun. Neither is very conducive to healing.

Holding my anger in won't help because . . .

84

As you explore what to do and as you make final decisions, find a companion who can help you evaluate the wisdom of your choices. Choose one who listens more than she talks, who hugs more than she prescribes. This person might be your sister, your father, your friend, your teacher—someone you can trust to want what's best for you. Share what happened and why it makes you mad. Explore together what you think God wants you to do about it. Look for specific ways God has already helped. Notice how just talking about your anger calms it, soothes your pain, and reminds you that God has provided people to care for you and help you master anger. Write the initials of family members or friends who might help you or who already have helped you: _____, _____, _____.

Consider the advice this person gives, or would give, for solving your present anger.

Once you've worked through your anger in detail, you don't necessarily have to go through the whole process every time angry feelings begin again. Here's a shorter exercise for defusing anger before it grabs hold.

Journaling Suggestions

God, I'm mad at _____ because . . .

My first reaction is to . . .

To make this reaction more healing, I . . .

I wish . . .

I'm glad I don't have to forget to forgive. Forgiving is

hard, but I know you'll help me to . . .

God, I think you want me to . . .

Leave It Behind

God has provided and will continue to provide ways out of your anger. Every time anger rears its head again, let him help you feel it, think and pray through it, burn off its energy, and decide what to do. Let pondering, thinking, praying, and reviewing heal your anger. Then move on. Leave anger behind where it belongs. You can't get to the healing without going through the anger, but you'll never reach the healing if you make your home in the middle of the anger.

CHAPTER **5**

I'll Never Feel Good Again

DISCOVER A PATH OUT OF DEPRESSION

It's been two months since my parents' divorce. I should be feeling better by now but I feel rotten. I'm tired all the time. I try to think but I feel thick-headed and dull. Things that usually come easily take forever to do. Activities that used to interest me hold no fascination. Nothing tastes good. Nothing looks real. Nothing feels right. Ever since my dad moved away I don't even feel like getting out of bed in the mornings. Why can't the world just stop, at least for a while?" asked Renee. "That seems the decent thing to do."

A new and deeper sadness hits a few days or weeks after the funeral, diagnosis, divorce, or other sad event. You've been through shock, sadness, guilt, and anger. All these experiences contribute to produce a deeper, more pervasive feeling called depression. This numbing sorrow makes it seem like you'll never feel good again. It is then that you must take one step at a time toward the light, even when you don't believe there's any light left.

Journaling Suggestions

Draw your current or most recent depression (deep sadness), focusing on the way it behaves. At what speed does your sadness move (slow and groggy like molasses; jumpy and touchy like a grouchy bear; surprisingly prickly like a rose; or what)?

What color is your depression?   What shape is your depression?

As you walk through your depression it may change speeds, colors, and shapes, but it will stay with you for a while. Rather than despair over this, get to know your sadness, the reasons for it, and the actions that ease it. Don't rush it. At the same time, notice as your sadness becomes less oppressive, as joy gradually overpowers it, as you develop the ability to participate in life again. Refuse to hold on to your depression after it's ready to go.

Even when you can't see any progress, hour by hour and day by day move through the despair and back into joy. No matter how slowly you move, you can move forward.

Notice God's Care

The hard part about moving through depression is the feeling that it's no use trying. The hole-in-your-chest pain is almost physical. You feel unable to breathe, to think, to complete sentences. You can't see even a twinkle of good in your future, let alone full-blown happiness. Depression makes you feel like you can never get better—but don't believe it. Depression is powerful, but it's always temporary. Recognize depression as a feeling that needs attention, not as a predictor of the future, your value, or your ability. Turn to God and the people he gives you for the power you need to make it through the dark days. You don't have to walk them alone.

During times of depression you may feel that God has deserted you. One reason for this is our tendency to associate God with joyful feelings. We think of him as a sensation of happiness or a gush of well-being. But God is a constant—he provides stability in the life-shaking disasters, joy in the good times, and understanding in both. You may not feel God, but he is most assuredly there. How do I know? Because he has promised to be.

> *And surely I will be with you always, to the very end of the age.*
>
> *Matthew 28:20*

> *And my God will meet all your needs according to his glorious riches in Christ Jesus.*
>
> *Philippians 4:19*

> *Even though I walk through the valley of the shadow of death, I will fear no evil, for you [God] are with me; your rod and your staff, they comfort me.*
>
> *Psalm 23:4*

God is there whether you feel him or not. Your body is just too sad to recognize him. God is walking right next to you, communicating his care with great intensity. Even when you can't feel or understand, know that God is there and the answers will come. You will make it through because God cares.

Did you know God says words like these to you when you are depressed?

✳ You are important to me.
✳ We'll make it through together.
✳ I care about your hurt. Tell me about it.
✳ What do you miss about him?
✳ I'm sad too.
✳ This is bad, but we can make it through together.
✳ One day all this pain will be over.

Journaling Suggestions

Doodle, draw, or describe God's presence with you and care of you.

Tap Into the Power

No matter how sad you feel, God will give you strength to go on living. This doesn't mean you'll immediately feel wonderful or that you'll find answers right away. It means you can move safely through the sadness to find a life worth living again. The Bible explains that going on sometimes means soaring, sometimes means running, and sometimes means simply putting one foot in front of the other.

> *Even youths grow tired and weary, and young men stumble and fall; but those who hope in the LORD will renew their strength. They will soar on wings like eagles; they will run and not grow weary, they will walk and not be faint.*
> *Isaiah 40:30–31*

Running is no less spiritual than soaring; walking is no less spiritual than running. Going on in any manner is a testimony to God's faithfulness and to your trust in him. It shows you're in touch with the one who will never desert you, that you're leaning on his strong arms. When something sad has happened, it's okay to feel unhappy. It's all right to feel tired, to go slowly, to stop and rest. Just keep moving. As you go on, keep in touch with God even when you can't think of what to say. He'll speak for you.

> *In the same way, the Spirit [God] helps us in our weakness. We do not know what we ought to pray, but the Spirit himself intercedes for us with groans that words cannot express.*
> *Romans 8:26*

Why are words unnecessary for some prayers? Draw or doodle a prayer you pray and the way God answers when you're deeply sad.

What's good about each way to go on during sadness?

Soaring—

Running—

Walking—

Draw a picture of yourself soaring, running, or walking during your present (or most recent) deep sadness.

Express How You Feel

Even after noticing that God cares and believing that he will get you through, you may still feel hopeless. That's okay. Despair is not logical. It's a feeling, and feelings pay little attention to reality. Even though hope is around the corner, you *feel* sad and that's all you can feel. Let depression do its work by letting yourself experience it for a time.

You may know exactly the reason for your depression, or you may not understand at all. Either way, as you feel the sadness and think it through, you'll discover actions that will pull you out of the despair. You may discover that you're angry about something; walk on through the anger rather than avoid it (see chapter 4). You may discover that you've never accepted God's forgiveness for something you did wrong, and you're still punishing yourself for it. Talk with God and a trusted Christian about this. Begin to live as a forgiven person (see chapter 3). You may discover that you're newly upset about something that hurt you in the past; take some time to be sad (see chapter 2). You may discover that you simply miss someone who's very important to you. Talk or write about how much you love that person. Then move on with God's power, waiting for the time when you'll see this one you love.

Whether you discover the specific reason for your depression or not, feeling it will help you heal. As you let yourself feel, express the feelings through talking, writing, thinking, composing, singing, drawing, painting, or whatever expression comes most naturally to you. Many people find it easier to compose when they're sad than at any other time.

Journaling Suggestions

Write a song or poem about the person or event you're sad about. You might want to write three verses, the first telling how bad you feel, the second telling how you begin to feel even worse, and the third telling the hope that gets you through your depression. Read Bible books like Lamentations and Psalms for ideas. If you prefer not to write a song, fill the space another way.

Verse 1:

Verse 2:

Verse 3:

Express your depression, and let it become a prayer. Here's
one a man named David wrote after confessing that he
had wronged both a woman and her husband:

Create in me a pure heart, O God,
and renew a steadfast spirit within me.
Do not cast me from your presence
or take your Holy Spirit from me.
Restore to me the joy of your salvation
and grant me a willing spirit, to sustain me.

Psalm 51:10-12

What does God say back to you as you tell him about your

sadness?

Some people dote on their sadness, even enjoy it. Name

reasons you might not want to feel better. Why is feeling

sadness and then leaving it behind the happier option?

Expect a Slower Pace

Going on during depression doesn't mean you skip through life as though nothing is any different. The person you care about or the event that has changed your life has impacted you deeply. While you adjust to the changes or get used to life without your loved one, things will be different. Start back into life bit by bit, gradually picking up speed. Because so much energy goes into feeling sad and adjusting to a different life, you will need extra time to do the things you usually do.

As an author I ordinarily write a chapter a week. But when my eleven-year-old daughter Emily was diagnosed with cancer, and during the two years she went through her excruciating chemotherapy, it took me up to four weeks to write a chapter. I had to take frequent breaks just to concentrate. I was impatient with my slowness and my constant grogginess. Bit by bit I recognized that I hurt so badly and my daughter hurt so badly, that I had little energy left for writing. Still I wouldn't, I couldn't, quit.

Why work at all? Because work brought the sense of normalcy I needed to survive. Work didn't get sick. It didn't die. It reminded me that I still had a brain, that I could still do something worthwhile, that the cancer couldn't take everything away from my daughter.

My husband and I sent Emily to school every day, even when I would have preferred to keep her home and cradle her in my arms, even when she would have preferred to stay in bed. Why go on with school and friendships and adventures when it was painful to do so? Because stopping had a pain of its own. If Emily went on, she had the chance of finding and enjoying something good. If she stopped, she had no opportunity to enjoy life. There were many times when she didn't think she could make it through the day. Sometimes she came home at noon. But interestingly, even on those days, she came home happy. A normal routine, coupled with friends who refused to let cancer get in the way of friendship, gave Emily strength to continue in spite of the pain. Sometimes we soared. Occasionally we ran. But most of the time we walked, one painful step at a time (Isaiah 40:31).

The chemotherapy side effects of baldness, aching joints, and plummeting moods were worse than any agony words can describe—but we persevered until we found God's joy poking its way through the pain. During those agonizing two years my daughter and I went through past, present, and future grief: grief about the past diagnosis, grief about the present side effects of chemotherapy, and grief about what might happen in the future. There was nothing easy about it. But we stubbornly determined that the cancer we hated was not going to steal the good in life. Even on the worst days we found something to enjoy. Today she's off chemo, her hair is back, and she is delighted to leave the cancer in her past.

Snatching the bits of joy that God sends—that's what going on in the midst of depression is all about. It's far from easy, but it's more than worth it. While waiting for painful chemotherapy treatments, Emily made friends with others in the waiting rooms. She joked with her doctor and nurses. These friendships brought joy in the midst of pain. They are gifts from God. Even when you feel no sense of drive or determination, keep on going. You'll notice that sad and happy blend in an uneasy but effective mix. And then the joy triumphs.

> *Because of the LORD's great love we are not consumed,*
> *for his compassions never fail.*
> *They are new every morning;*
> *great is your faithfulness.*
> *Lamentations 3:22–23*

Journaling Suggestions

Write your story of going on even when you were sad.

Describe something good that came (or could come) in the

midst of it.

Write or doodle about the things you find hardest to do when you're depressed (think, talk, work, learn, play, and so on). The footprints are there to remind you that you and God will make it one step at a time.

Take a Break

Going on during depression does not mean you never stop—it means you stop occasionally rather than permanently. After each of Emily's chemotherapy treatments, our family went away for the weekend. Together with God, we did something fun to distract from the pain and then huddled together to manage the pain we could not distract. These retreats strengthened all four of us—Emily, Emily's sister, my husband, and me. Through them God gave us the power we needed to go on.

Journaling Suggestions

Circle your favorite way to retreat.

❖ Write in my diary   ❖ Go somewhere with my family

❖ Sleep   ❖ Be alone in my room

❖ Listen to music

❖ Participate in a church retreat

❖ Talk with a close friend   ❖ Think

❖ Read a good book

❖ Work on my car, garden, or _____

❖ Draw, compose, or create in another way

❖ View or hear someone else's creation

❖ Do something exciting   ❖ Do something quiet

❖ Stay home   ❖ Just sit and be

❖ _____

Draw or describe the place you retreat to and what you do

while you're there.

Watch How You Treat Others

Depression is a pause for healing, not an excuse for acting however you want to act. For too many people, depression goes like this:

> *Be touchy and tell people you can't help treating them badly because you feel rotten. Whine and complain and take your frustration out on everybody near you. Make sure everyone feels super sorry for you, dotes on you, and grants your every whim. Enjoy the attention so much that you stay sad long after you could have gotten better. Refuse to notice anyone else's need, even if they are grieving for the same person or situation.*

Granted, your energy is low and it takes more effort to be kind, but use whatever energy it takes to show caring. Fully experience your feelings, but don't torment those around you. Refuse to use your depression as an excuse for lashing out or as a tool for getting attention. Resist creating more depression by acting cruelly. Even when you're sad, be kind. You don't have to bubble over, but do refrain from snapping. Besides the fact that cruelty is wrong, even the best of friends will tire of your constant focus on yourself. Rather than selfishly wallow in your depression, care for others. Not only is this good for the people around you—caring for others actually helps you heal more quickly.

Depression seldom starts as selfishness. It's usually simple sadness. But the attention you get from depression can make you want to stay there. Realize that there are better ways to get attention—ways like mutual love and genuine care.

Refuse Suicide

Having suicidal feelings doesn't make you weird or morbid. It means you're sad. The deep, debilitating sadness of depression makes you feel like you can't go on. This vulnerable and scary feeling makes death seem better than the pain.

You just want the hurting to stop. But suicide neither heals nor stops the sadness; your death will just perpetuate it. Only by walking through the sadness can you end the pain.

Many of us have a romantic image of suicide: The pain will go away and we can keep on enjoying the good. But once you die, you have no hope of joy on earth. And you'll create tremendous grief for the people around you. Refuse suicide, knowing that there's no return from this path. Decide to walk on through the despair to the hope on the other side. Take it one day at a time, refusing to even think about tomorrow. When suicidal feelings come, recognize them but refuse to fulfill them.

Journaling Suggestions

Why do you think so many people choose suicide?

Why do many people who feel like committing suicide choose to live instead?

Below are some tools for managing depression and dealing with suicidal feelings. Doodle ways you could do each. Then try to add an idea of your own.

1. *Know God cares.* Even when you can't feel him, and even when it seems like no other human being gives a flip, God cares personally for you: *I have loved you with an everlasting love; I have drawn you with loving-kindness. I will build you up again and you will be rebuilt (Jeremiah 31:3–4).*

2. *Find an adult or same-age friend who will listen and understand.* If you feel like fulfilling your suicidal feelings, tell this to someone you trust. You don't have to fight the feelings on your own.

3. *Recognize your value as a person created by God.* Whenever anyone commits suicide, it shakes the community. You matter to God and to other people. Refuse to believe otherwise.

4. *Make it through one more day.* Deep sadness can make even that seem like a big job. Refuse to look at forever, or even next week. Focus only on today.

107

5. *Post Bible promises.* Put them around your room or keep them in your purse or billfold.

6. *Write, draw, or talk about your feelings.* Refuse to hold them inside. This lets out some of the sadness.

7. *Remember that God understands.* He has felt the feelings you feel (see Hebrews 2:17–18).

8. *Assume that this day is not typical.* Other days won't feel this bad.

9. *Read Bible books that tell about happy endings after sad times.* These include Lamentations, Psalms, and Habakkuk. Notice that it took time for happiness to come again, but it came.

10. *List reasons you have to live.* Chapter 7 will help you do this. Examples include: my death won't bring my brother back; my parents would miss me; I have a brain that could be used for good; somebody I haven't met yet needs me.

Choose to Live

Choose not only to stay alive but to really *live,* to find and enjoy the good in life, to openly care for the people around you. It's seldom easy to go on living during depressing days, but only by going on can you move from pain to peace. When pain comes to you, as it already has and invariably will again, choose life (recall Deuteronomy 30:19–20).

Yes, it hurts. But hurting now doesn't mean you'll hurt forever. You can walk through the darkness to the light on the other side. When you're in the middle, you can't see any light, but it's there. Just keep walking toward it. What makes it easiest for you to know there's hope at the end of the tunnel? How will you choose life?

* I've been through pain before.
  * A friend reminds me that I'm going to make it.
    * God assures me of his presence.
      * I feel the love and support of my family.
        * I've watched someone else make it through.
          * I feel a hope that persists even in the darkest of days.

* _____

As you grieve and heal, move on with life. Stay at least minimally involved with life while your body and soul grieve. It may take weeks. It may take days. It may take minutes. But joy will come again. Go on through the pain, confident that the only way to the joy is through the tunnel. You can make it.

CHAPTER 6

Why Did God Let This Happen?

FIND TRUE ANSWERS TO TRAGEDY

I'm only sixteen years old," said Jerry. "How can I have cancer? I've taken care of myself, I've never smoked or taken drugs, and I don't live around toxic chemicals. Maybe God is punishing me for something—I can think of lots of stuff I've done wrong, but I can't remember anything I did that was bad enough to deserve cancer. Maybe the flu or a broken leg, but cancer? I'm so afraid. Maybe if I'm super good these next few months I'll be cured."

Why is God mad at Jerry? He's not. Jerry's cancer is a product of the imperfect world we live in. God no more gave the cancer to Jerry than a mother would give poison to her child. So why is Jerry upset? Jerry, as a famous author describes it, has God pictured as a big "candy machine in the sky." If we put in coins of goodness he delivers health, protection, and good events; if we put in bad behavior he delivers illness, trouble, tragedy, or pain.

This sounds right and fair. But I'm not so sure we'd like it if we got it. First of all, it detaches God, making him an impersonal and cold force rather than the warm and tenderly loving caregiver he is. It makes us want to use God rather than love him. It ultimately turns spirituality into a selfish pursuit—we choose good only because it gets us something. "Sure I'll be a Christian: It's great 'fire insurance,' and it'll keep me safe here on earth too. I'll never have a problem or an illness."

The candy-machine mentality also promotes fear rather than closeness. If we have to behave to keep God from punishing us, we won't feel very loving toward him. We'll worry that we can never live up to his standard. We'll hesitate to talk to him in case our thoughts or ideas offend him. We'll want to hide from God rather than draw near to him. This mentality sees goodness as a burden, something we do only because the Big Man in the Sky is watching. It's better to do good because it shows our trust in God and our love for people. It's also better to do good because it's the right thing to do.

Finally, we don't really want what we deserve. When we're honest we admit that we've all used people to get what we want, we've had some pretty mean thoughts and actions, and we've lashed out when we should have acted with kindness. Fortunately, God loves us anyway. He looks past the bad to see the good, past our present to see our potential. He notices the hopes behind our hesitations, the feelings behind our failures, the skills behind our shortcomings. With this foundation of unconditional love, he gently whittles away our weaknesses and builds up our strengths. This refining process does not mean he brings death or disaster into our lives. Instead he takes both the good and bad and uses them as raw material to build strong character in us (see Romans 5:3–5).

The main problem with do-good-and-I'll-get-good is that it's simply not true. God's not sitting in heaven waiting to catch us doing wrong so he can zap us. Nor does he put magical bubbles of protection around his people, though we wish he would. Instead God becomes intimately involved with the lives of those who will let him in. He points out actions that bring joy and shows us how to live those actions. He warns us about deceptive paths that look good but lead to misery. He tries to steer us around dangers and disasters. He rejoices with us when things go well and weeps with us when tragedies come. He offers his power to combat the crises and his security to get us through despair. For reasons not totally understood, these gifts are better and stronger than protection from pain.

Journaling Suggestions

How do you view God? How has your understanding of him changed over the years? Draw your impression of an incomplete view of God, such as a genie who grants our every wish, a big grandfather in the sky, a scorekeeper, or a good luck charm.

Now use this page to draw or describe God as he really is.

Ask Your Questions

If God is personal and loving, it seems as though he'd use his power to cure a few diseases and prevent a few tragic deaths for his faithful people. Wouldn't a caring God stop the pain? Why does God let so many bad things happen?

I don't know the complete answer, but I do understand bits of it. The better I understand God, the easier it is to live with unanswered questions. I do know that God agonizes over each individual who suffers, dies, or cries. But God restrains himself because of a gift called freedom. Apparently he knows about a bigger agony—being controlled. To stop Ted's van just before it flipped would take away Ted's freedom to learn confidence that's not threatened by dares. If God controlled what we did, said, and chose, our actions would become irrelevant. Even if we stepped off a cliff, God would catch us before we hit the bottom. My compliments to a friend would mean nothing because God *made* me say kind things. God's constant intervention would make us little more than puppets in a meaningless world. We need a consistent place with routines we can count on, where up is up and down is down, where hugs mean care, and smiles mean you're important to me.

God's control would take away our ability to choose, a gift we humans cherish. Rather than orchestrate each little detail of the world, God has set the world in motion and trusted us to run it well or poorly. He doesn't abandon us— he stays involved by offering his direction and his power for finding and living the good. He explains the laws of nature, the laws of people, and the laws of love so we'll understand why cars shouldn't drive off cliffs and people shouldn't say cruel words to each other. Then he lets us choose how things will go. Certainly if we obeyed God consistently, things would go a lot more smoothly here on earth. But we don't. We've made a grand mess of things so that even those who try to do good now reap the consequences of others' cruelty.

In his foreknowledge, God knew this would happen—why did he allow it? Somehow he must know it's worth it.

I'd certainly like God to fix the evil, wipe out the diseases, obliterate the cruelty. But if he did, we would lose freedom. We would never know true human love because people would have no choice about loving us. We would never experience the triumph of success after striving to achieve, because God would have done it for us. Knowing the value of love, triumph, and more, God has given us the freedom to choose.

Unfortunately, people have taken their freedom to love and used it to hurt each other. Some people use their freedom to neglect or abuse their children. Why does God allow it? So parents can choose to truly nurture their children.

Some people have chosen to trivialize human life. Human choice leads to the murder of convenience store workers for a few lousy dollars. Why does God allow the choice? So people can build genuine trust and real caring.

Some people have taken the freedom to have true fun and replaced it with empty fun. They drive fast, use alcohol, or abuse drugs. These actions bring indescribable misery to millions of people. Why does God allow it? So people can choose sincere fun and real laughter.

Rather than care for the world, people have polluted it with toxic chemicals, creating an environment that may bring cancer to innocent teenagers like Jerry. Why does God allow it? So people can choose to grow flowers, plant corn, and create healthy surroundings.

Some suffering can't be traced to human causes. Babies are born with birth defects. Volcanoes wipe out cities. Why? Romans 8:18–25 explains that it has something to do with the imperfection of our world.

I imagine God has to sit on his hands to keep from stopping each incident of suffering. I see his tears as he feels our pain. For the sake of good, he doesn't stop the bad. Instead he offers something better: security and power that surpass the most distressing disabilities, diseases, and deaths. The security and power don't make the pain go away, nor do they make the injustices okay, but they do help us pass through them until we get to the perfection of heaven.

God then pokes good gifts into the darkness. He doesn't wait until bad times come to do this; he simply continues to give the good he's been giving all along. He refuses to let sadness have the last word. God's steady care is the one constant you can count on through every experience of your life. He gives you people, circumstances, and power to make it through the roughest times and to enjoy the best ones. Notice God's provision, his power, his consistency in your life. He's the one person you can always count on. Recognize the good God is bringing to your darkness.

Journaling Suggestions

The problem of pain is not a logical or easy one. The way God loves is hard to define or describe, but it's very real. How do you understand the love of God in the middle of your pain? Draw or verbalize your insights.

Draw or describe a time God's power, security, and

consistency got you through a sad time (maybe right now).

Draw or describe good gifts God pokes into your life, no

matter how deep or long-lasting the pain.

Sadness comes to all of us. Death or other tragedy is not

a punishment for something you did or didn't do. It's

simply part of life in this world. You can use your God-

given freedom to show love to those who are hurting.

Describe or draw a way you'll use your freedom to bring

joy into someone's life rather than pain.

Keep Asking until You Understand

Even after thinking things through, questions about suffering may still bother you. Christians have struggled with the problem of pain and suffering for centuries. Even after all these years the answers are seldom perfectly clear or flawlessly complete. But the answers can still satisfy. My eight-year-old daughter Sarah must struggle to hear every conversation because of severe hearing loss. She doesn't like the hearing loss, and she knows there's nothing good about it, but she does like the fact that God will help her hurdle the obstacles. She finds ways to speak clearly, to hear her friend with the high-pitched voice, to understand her teacher in a noisy classroom. The answer that satisfies is the certainty that God is on her side, the assurance that she'll never face the challenges alone. No answer about *why* she has poor hearing feels good. Neither she nor I like the fact that an imperfect world means imperfections in our bodies. But we both have confidence that heaven means hearing clearly again. We trust that God will help Sarah make friends, succeed in school, and find places where she belongs. Barring a miracle, she'll never be able to whisper with her girlfriends or converse without hearing aids. But we refuse to let hearing loss steal the joy of living. The answers are incomplete, but God is complete. We find satisfaction and confidence in God and his insurmountable power. God, not the answers, gets us through.

Some people say we shouldn't question God, that such mysteries are not meant for us to understand. Certainly God understands better than we do, but it's never wrong to ask God questions. If a question bothers you, it's important to both you and God. Asking shows you trust God to have and give the answers. Questions become bad only when we use them as excuses for not trusting or obeying God. Pursue your questions until you find *real* answers, answers that help you move through your grief, heal your anger, cleanse you from guilt, and equip you to care about those around you. As you ask, there are three actions that can help.

1. *Recognize that God cares and is the giver of good gifts.* If we know God is on our side, we can fight the problem with him. We don't have to figure out why God would hurt us, because he wouldn't.

> *When tempted, no one should say, "God is tempting me."*
> *For God cannot be tempted by evil, nor does he tempt any-*
> *one . . . Don't be deceived, my dear brothers. Every good*
> *and perfect gift is from above, coming down from the Father*
> *of the heavenly lights, who does not change like shifting*
> *shadows.*
>
> James 1:13, 16–17

God cares for you. He's not out to get you. Sad things don't happen as punishment or because God has singled you out. They're a part of the world we live in and they come to everyone, good and bad (see Matthew 5:45). Some bad things happen because of personal choice: Car accidents occur when someone chooses to drive while drunk or doesn't look where she's going. Some bad things happen because of a complex network of choices: Cancer occurs when generations of people corrupt the environment with carcinogenic chemicals and pollution. Some bad things happen because of the incompleteness and imperfection of the world itself. No human makes muscular dystrophy or earthquakes. They're distortions of good on this flawed planet we call earth (see Romans 8:18-25 and 1 John 1:5).

2. *Give it a rest.* Struggling with questions of life and death, cause and effect, faith and doubt takes lots of energy. Don't spend all your healing energy on asking why. After pondering for a while, move on to something else. An insight may come when you're not even thinking about the question. Too often we spend so much time wondering *why* the

death or illness or accident happened that we can't ask the more important question: What do I do now?

3. *Focus on questions you can do something about.* Even if you understood exactly why something happened to you, you still wouldn't want it to be happening. Instead of "Why?" focus on "What actions will help me through this rough time?" Instead of "What is the answer?" focus on "Where does the power come from?" Nobody likes death, illness, disability, or tragedy, but when they come we can lean on God's everlasting arms, heal through his loving care, and tap into his power for going on with life. Together with God, discover the actions that heal you, equip you to cope, and guide you toward joy in the midst of every circumstance.

Journaling Suggestions

Write questions you have for God. Jot or doodle your current insights, and then add insights as you discover them in the days to come. Talk with caring Christians, search the Bible, observe how your life unfolds. The answers are there because The Answer, God himself, is real and he cares.

Evaluate What You Hear

As we seek answers, wise Christian friends can help. But some well-meaning Christians give answers that sound good but don't match God or the Bible. Here are some commonly given answers that have been repeated through the ages. See if you can spot the shortcoming in each before reading on. Write or illustrate your response and then a more biblical answer in the space provided.

You shouldn't question God.

Contrary to popular opinion, God likes questions. Questions show you have confidence in God and you want to learn from him. Just as you ask the smart kid at school, ask God because you trust him to have the answers. Attitude has much to do with the value of a question—some questions are shouts of anger rather than genuine requests for information—but as rage calms, we become open to real answers.

God gave this to you so you'd be stronger in your faith.

We can't say why God does what he does. But the Bible indicates that God does not send sad or trying circumstances—he responds to them. God doesn't give bad things to make us strong, to test our faith, or to strengthen our characters, because he doesn't give bad things at all. Instead in the midst of handicaps he provides opportunities to triumph.

In the midst of injustice he gives motivation to right the wrongs. He recasts death into a passage to new life. In every circumstance he furnishes us with skills to find good in the midst of the horror. The bad never becomes good. But God refuses to let wrong have the last word (see Genesis 50:20).

God gave this to you because you're such a strong Christian.

Death, diseases, and disabilities aren't rewards for good behavior. They're a result of living in an imperfect world, a world marred by sin and selfishness. God doesn't give troubles to those who are already strong; he gives strength to those who have troubles. Before Jesus left the earth he explained to his disciples: *I have told you these things, so that in me you may have peace. In this world you will have trouble. But take heart! I have overcome the world (John 16:33).*

125

Bad things bring out the best in us.

God doesn't have to wait for evil to bring good. He works to bring good all the time. It's just as much a miracle when faith grows during good times as in bad. Examples of good that grows during happy times are clear thinking, appreciation, kindness, friendliness, and service. Sad times leave little energy for service or clear thinking. But sad times can help us develop endurance, patience, and perspective. They whittle away the petty and trivial. Many people grow during sad times; but there are others who become bitter during sadness. They turn away from God, angry at him for causing the event or refusing to stop it. Many people grow during good times, but others take credit for their own good fortune and decide they don't need God. All events in life bring the opportunity for growth.

Don't be sad. He's in heaven. A true Christian isn't sad for long.

Sadness is not contrary to faith; it's an expression of love (see John 11:35–36). Death, tragedy, illness, and disability are insults to the goodness of God. To agonize over them shows we know they're not right. As we cry over sad events and mourn the results of bad choices, we gain the strength to go on and to reclaim joy. We let our confidence in God's goodness bring lasting healing.

Many people in church fear pain. They want us to be instantly better and they worry when we frown. But sadness is a godly response to sad things (see Ecclesiastes 3:4). True healing takes time. Romans 12:15 encourages us to rejoice with those who rejoice and mourn with those who mourn.

God never makes mistakes. You've got to accept this as God's will.

It is very true that God doesn't make mistakes, but people do. The car accident that killed Rand and injured Kelly was a human mistake. God no more orchestrated this than a loving father would torture his child. Not everything that happens on earth is God's perfect will. When we say something is God's will, we must carefully define what we mean by that. God's will has many facets, and the first of these is his perfect will. In God's perfect will no person would hurt another. No one would die. Everyone would live forever in loving fellowship with God and with other believers. But we humans have marred the world by choosing to sin. We have chosen to hurt each other, hurt ourselves, and hurt God. The pain we feel is a direct or indirect consequence of these choices. Herein lies God's permissive will—he wills that we make our own choices. Some of these choices, choices God does not approve of, bring pain and sadness. Pain and sadness are not God's perfect

127

will, and he grieves when we cause them. God wants life, unity, caring, safety, and growth. He offers his guidance to find this happy path, but too often we ignore him. We choose dares, cuts, cruelty, or disease-causing habits. Human choice brought the death that now impacts all of us. Human choice continues the cruelty and self-centeredness that hurts us from day to day.

So what is the answer? God himself is the answer. We don't have to articulate his hows or whys. We can simply lean on him. Then we can use our human choice to redeem at least some of the sadness caused by others. When death hits, we survivors can rally around to fill in some of the love gaps left by the one who died. When someone acts cruelly, we can respond with the positive care that heals. When we're tempted to act in a self-centered way, we can choose to think of the other person's thoughts and feelings. We can let God love through us by saying things like, "I'm sorry you have cancer" and "What can I do to help?"

128

As you search for answers, remember that just because a Christian says it doesn't make it so. God acts as God acts, not as we want him to or as we think he should.

Journaling Suggestions

Write an answer you heard during sadness that made you feel worse instead of better. Then substitute an answer that matches the Bible and that really works.

Hurting words

Helping words

"Don't worry or be sad."

"How are you feeling about it?"

"You've got to accept it."

"This is really hard, isn't it?"

Write a letter that answers Jerry's questions at the beginning of the chapter.

Dear Jerry,

Embrace Your Friend

We don't need a firmly worked-out answer as much as we need a God we can depend on, someone who can't be taken away from us.

> *For he himself is our peace, who has made the two one and has destroyed the barrier, the dividing wall of hostility . . . And in him you too are being built together to become a dwelling in which God lives by his Spirit.*
>
> *Ephesians 2:14, 22*

Jesus promises that he'll give us peace and take care of us in every situation. Just before he died and went to heaven he explained to his disciples:

> *Peace I leave with you; my peace I give you. I do not give to you as the world gives. Do not let your hearts be troubled and do not be afraid.*
>
> *John 14:27*

131

When troubles come, our lives can be turned upside down and our thoughts confused, but our hearts don't have to be. We can know without a shadow of a doubt that God cares, and because God cares we'll make it through. He will take care of us, both now and forever. We are secure no matter what happens. Jesus is not fickle—he is the one unchanging, steady constant in our lives. We can trust him. He is always there for us and he will meet all our needs.

Draw, doodle, describe, or depict your confidence in God.

Journaling Suggestions

Why is he himself your answer?

CHAPTER 7

I Don't Think I Can Make It

GET THROUGH THE ROUGH SPOTS

I don't know if I can make it," confided Theo. "My dad died last month, and everything around here has been weird ever since. Mom stays busy all the time, maybe in an effort to avoid the memories. She's tired when she gets home, so there's never anybody here for me. I'm lonely and sad and no one seems to know I exist. I tried romance, but girls just use me and then dump me. Friends think I'm lucky to have all this freedom. They don't understand what it's like. Sometimes I wonder if God even cares. I might as well just kill myself. That would be one less person for Mom to worry about and one less person for the world to be bothered by."

Theo's despondency is understandable. He feels like every door he tries brings pain. He has lost both parents, one to death and one to busyness. Neither girls nor friends have shown love for him. It's a lonely, scary time. But Theo is not trapped. There are more doors to open. He can find belonging again. As he waits out the time his mother needs to recover, he can find caring adults who will fill in his parenting needs. He can find friends who genuinely like him, who need his abilities, who want his company. These people may be at church, at school, or where he works, but they are there. How do I know? Because God will provide them. God cares personally, even when Theo can't feel him.

God knows we need love, belonging, security, and purpose. We need avenues for giving and a reason for living. When one doorway closes, he provides others.

> *"For I know the plans I have for you," declares the* LORD, *"plans to prosper you and not to harm you, plans to give you hope and a future. Then you will call upon me and come and pray to me, and I will listen to you. You will seek me and find me when you seek me with all your heart."*
> *Jeremiah 29:11–13*

> *I will not leave you as orphans; I will come to you.*
> *John 14:18*

> *The* LORD *appeared to us in the past, saying: "I have loved you with an everlasting love; I have drawn you with loving-kindness. I will build you up again and you will be rebuilt . . . Again you will . . . go out to dance with the joyful."*
> *Jeremiah 31:3–4*

134

Draw or describe the love someone gave you when you were grieving over death, divorce, diagnosis, or another sad event.

That love was a gift from God. He cares for you both through people and through wrapping his own arms around you. If you can't remember anyone caring, look around now. God's people-gifts are there—recognize them.

Decide to Keep Going

Making it through grief is ultimately a decision. Theo must decide to survive, to find joy again even with people missing in his life. He won't feel good instantly, but he will eventually. Theo can choose to do whatever needs doing to get through the hard times. Theo has seen his friend Tony overcome physical disability and create happiness in spite of it. Tony refuses to let his wheelchair get in the way of life. Because Theo realizes his emotional obstacle is similar, he decides to overcome his loneliness. He commits to develop relationships with people who care about him, people in whose lives he can make a difference.

As Theo makes friends who genuinely care rather than use him, he develops the relationships he needs to feel loved. As he joins groups and tries new activities, he develops the confidence he needs to make it in the world. As he looks forward to reunion with his father he finds joy in life. Both Theo and Tony decide to get on with life rather than moan about how they wish things could be.

This is more than sheer determination. It's depending on God, the ultimate source of security and joy. It's recognizing that pain is a part of life, but not the only part. It's looking past the agony to find the pleasure. It's understanding that the walk toward light is a journey rather than instant success.

Know You're Not Alone

In the midst of his despair, Theo feels certain that no one could feel as badly as he does. Feeling alone in suffering compounds his sadness. It may help Theo to realize tough times

135

come to everyone. They come in different forms, but they come to us all. Problems have been here since Adam and Eve and will stay until Jesus returns. God assures us through the Bible that problems are part of life, not a signal that something is wrong or that God has abandoned us.

> *Dear friends, do not be surprised at the painful trial you are suffering, as though something strange were happening to you.*
>
> *1 Peter 4:12*

The passage goes on to offer this advice:

> *So then, those who suffer according to God's will should commit themselves to their faithful Creator and continue to do good.*
>
> *1 Peter 4:19*

136

Rather than worry about why his life is hard right now, Theo can continue to serve God by doing good. He can determine to make it through the pain to the easy parts on the other side. It's never fun to go through a sad time, but Theo can make it. Notice two important facts:

1. *Suffering is part of life on this earth.* It's not a welcome part, but it's a part we all experience. This fact won't instantly take away Theo's pain. But it can assure him that he's not the only one suffering, nor has he been singled out to hurt. Theo can look around and find people who seem to have it better, but then he'll feel abused. He can look around and find people who seem to have worse problems, but then he might feel smug. Instead, Theo must choose to simply get through his own pain.

2. *Living according to God's will prevents some suffering.* As Theo obeys God he'll spread joy rather than create more pain. For instance, Theo can listen to his mom rather

than grump at her, smile at friends rather than scowl, compliment the good rather than criticize the bad, say "I need some time alone right now" rather than "Get out of my face!" He can choose friends who bring out the best in him, who value him, who give to him as well as take from him. If Theo has shown kindness during his good times, friends are more likely to respond with the care Theo needs. If not, he can start that kindness now. These actions will decrease the severity of the suffering he can't change and will prevent future suffering.

Why not just give up? Because the good times are just as real and persistent as the bad ones. If we give up, we bypass the good. Good and bad come side by side, hand in hand. We decide which hand we'll take—despair or hope.

Journaling Suggestions

Illustrate or describe a time during which you felt like giving up. Who was around or not around? What had just happened? How long did your despair last? Do you still feel this way? If not, what or who changed your feeling?

God's love for you gives you security. Draw this love in the way you experience it.

God will take care of you no matter how bad things get by providing people and experiences to give you joy, and by guiding you to become a joy giver. From the list below, check off reasons your life is worth living. Identify at least three reasons you'll choose life rather than death. Then add reasons of your own.

[ ] Nobody can replace the one who died. But God will take care of me by giving me other people who care.

[ ] There are many things in life I haven't tried yet.

[ ] God will give me something to live for.

[ ] If I die, I won't be around to enjoy _____.

[ ] I've made it through sad times before, and good came.

[ ] I like living.

[ ] I can keep in touch with my friend who moved.

[ ] I can continue the good that my dead friend left undone.

[ ] If I live, I could prevent somebody else from wanting to die. I could make this world a better place.

[ ] If I kill myself I won't get to see who comes to my funeral. I'll end my chances of making friends.

[ ] I feel like nobody cares, but if I live a little longer, somebody might like me someday.

[ ] God has a specific purpose for me. If I quit life early, that job will go undone and those people will go unloved.

[ ]

Embrace L.I.F.E.

Take definite steps to choose life. Act on the following four principles to make it through your dark days.

Life Matters

No matter how you feel right now, your life matters. Do you remember the movie "It's a Wonderful Life"? The first time I watched it, I thought the movie had been mistitled. Everything went wrong for George, the main character in the story. He never got to fulfill his lifelong dream of travel and adventure. First he lost the hearing in his left ear rescuing his kid brother. Then his father died just as George was about to leave home. George stayed to temporarily run his father's business, a building and loan that helped nearly every family in town. His brother had promised to take over later but reneged on his commitment, leaving George there a little longer. Finally even the business George had poured his life into failed. In his despair he considered jumping into the river—but then he saved someone else who fell in first. Later he wished he had never been born at all. Suddenly everything changed, and George was shown what life would have been like without him. The villain whom George had held in check took over the town. George's wife spent her life as a lonely librarian. His mother lived in poverty. George discovered that his life, quite different from what he had originally hoped, had made a difference. He had brought good to the world simply by caring for his family and friends.

You can do the same. You fill a place that belongs uniquely to you. You have people around you who need your special brand of care. You may not have cared for people in the past, but you can start now. Look around to see the people who might need your friendliness, who might want your ideas, who might benefit from your experience. Now give yourself to them, small action by small action, in the name of Jesus Christ.

How is your life different than you thought it would be? What good is happening anyway? You may feel your life doesn't matter because you've caused more pain than joy, that the world would be better off without you. Suppose you, like Ted, were driving the car that killed your friend. Is it fair that you should live if he can't? Of course it's not fair—because any one death is too many. But taking your life will only perpetuate the pain. If you die, your community will have lost two friends. If you live on, you can do some of the good your dead friend can no longer do. No matter what your circumstances, you can make the world a better place by genuinely caring about the well-being of everyone around you.

If you've never seen the movie, watch it: It will encourage you more than any words of mine can.

It Happens in Tiny Steps

You don't have to feel instantly good to make progress. Recovery from sad experiences happens gradually but certainly. A first step is to notice the good that still exists. When something sad happens you feel like everything has collapsed. But there's always some structure left. When Jerry got cancer, he still had a family that loved him, a family he could share both good times and bad times with. When Melanie's grandfather died she still had all the understanding skills he had taught her, skills she could use with her friends and family members. When Kelly's legs were paralyzed, she still had the use of her arms. When Sarah lost her hearing, she still had clear sight and a ready smile. When Theo's dad died, he still had a smart brain and a yearning for excellence.

A second step is to use those positive elements to create joy in your life. Jerry leaned on his family during the excruciating chemotherapy, and they rejoiced together when he was cured. Melanie became known as a friend who cared and would never betray anyone. Kelly used her arms to maneuver her wheelchair with speed and dexterity. Sarah's smile made people forget all about her hearing loss. Theo chose to become a medical researcher who just might find a cure for the illness that stole his father's life.

All this is not to say that the sad events don't matter. They do. But there is always something to live for, no matter how precious the previous reason was. Hopelessness is a pervasive emotion that tries to seep through all of life. Refuse to let it do this by plugging the holes with hope. When you have a disaster in your love life, notice that your friendships are going well and let these friends help you through the romantic crisis. When one of your friends goes through a trauma, let your family help you cope. When both friends and family abandon you, draw on the inner strength God has built in you to make more friends who become like family.

Feelings Are Indicators, Not Dictators

There's nothing wrong with feeling like not going on; it's a symptom of depression. There *is* something wrong with letting that feeling dictate what happens to you. If you let the feeling rule, you'll end up dead. If you respond to the feeling, you'll end up happy. Respond to depression by sleeping, by writing or otherwise expressing your feelings, by talking, by simply being, by deciding what to do next (see chapters 2 and 5 for more ideas).

Mikki felt horribly guilty after having sex with several boyfriends. "Each time I thought it was really love. But each time our relationship deteriorated and I felt used." Mikki can't undo this mistake, and she knows it. She never considered suicide, but she unwittingly participated in other self-punishing behavior—she let her grades slip, withdrew from parties and other social gatherings, stopped going to church, quit laughing, and refused to believe that anything she did was worthwhile. Her guilt helped no one, including herself. Mikki let her feelings rule rather than listen to what they indicated: the need for forgiveness and a lifestyle change. As Mikki seeks forgiveness and lives like the quality person God created her to be, she'll begin to feel worthwhile. She'll refuse to let guys use her sexually or in any other way. She'll enjoy her next sexual sharing on her wedding night.

Feelings let us know that something is wrong and needs attention. Give that need attention. Decide to respond to your feelings rather than let them rule you.

Everybody Needs Somebody

You need people to help you through, and people need you to help them through. Even when you don't think there's a single soul in the universe who cares about you, *people care*. God places people in your path to give you encouragement, love, skills, and hope. This person may be someone you've known a long time but have never noticed. It may be someone new. It may be a parent or other family member you've loved since birth. Recognize these people. And notice when you are the person God is placing in another's path.

Kelly gets support from her dad. He listens with understanding and compassion. He gives her all the time she needs to talk things out and think things through. Sometimes they sit in the same room doing different things, but his care is obvious.

Ted's dad is better at lecturing than listening, so he turns to his grandmother. They talk while she works puzzles with him.

Theo has no family member that shows him care, but he's developing two friendships at church, one with an adult and one with a boy his age. The adult has a ready smile and sends

143

notes of encouragement. The peer blends humor with understanding as he refuses to let Theo miss any youth activities.

These caregivers hug instead of prescribe, wait instead of push, respond instead of react. Look around for the parents, grandparents, adult friends, same-age friends, younger children, teachers, and other caregivers God has placed in your path.

Journaling Suggestions

Many of us get support from the people who were already in our lives before the crisis hits. Others seek someone new—a professional counselor, a pastor, or a neutral person who can see the situation objectively. Write the initials of people from whom you have received or will receive support:

_____ _____ _____

Write or doodle why you will not only go on with life but will embrace life at its fullest. Respond to these four areas, but don't feel bound by them.

My Life is important because . . .

In tiny steps, I'll notice the good of _____ and let this good create joy by . . .

My Feelings indicate the need for . . .

Because I'm an Everybody who needs somebody, I'll turn to _____ for . . .

Because I can be somebody another person needs, I'll

help _____ by . . .

Now write two stories, the first about what happens when

you decide the death, diagnosis, or disability is too great

and you quit on life.

Write a second story in which you decide to live, both for
your sake and for the sake of the people around you.

Which story would you rather live, and why? Which story
do you think the people around you would rather see
happen? Why?

Help Someone Else Go On

One of the best ways to recover from a sad event is to give at least some of your time to help someone else. Because you've felt pain, you're uniquely qualified to offer sensitivity, understanding, and care. You won't give pat answers or try to whisk away pain with a cliché. You can even help a friend or family member through the same rough time you're going through right now. The two of you can work together to manage the pain, neither of you carrying the full load by yourself.

You may be the reason someone else chooses to go on with life. You can make a difference.

Praise be to the God and Father of our Lord Jesus Christ, the Father of compassion and the God of all comfort, who comforts us in all our troubles, so that we can comfort those in any trouble with the comfort we ourselves have received from God. For just as the sufferings of Christ flow over into our lives, so also through Christ our comfort overflows.
2 Corinthians 1:3–5

Carry each other's burdens, and in this way you will fulfill the law of Christ.
Galatians 6:2

Let us not give up meeting together, as some are in the habit of doing, but let us encourage one another—and all the more as you see the Day approaching.
Hebrews 10:25

148

Journaling Suggestions

Write the initials of a family member or friend who may feel like he or she can't make it: _____. Why does he or she feel so sad?

[ ] Someone dear has died

[ ] Someone has been mean or thoughtless

[ ] He or she was cut from the team

[ ] Family problems

[ ] Friendship or romance problems

[ ] Serious illness in self or someone close

[ ] Did poorly on a test or other important event

[ ] _____

[ ] _____

What concrete expressions of love from you might ease the despair? What actions might cause it to worsen? Circle actions that might help your friend. Then add some of your own.

☞ Ask: "How are things going?" and then listen if she

feels like talking.

☞ Spend time silently if she doesn't feel like talking.

☞ Send little gifts that show you care.

☞ Help catch up at school or do chores.

☞ Stay involved and interested in her.

☞ Let her tell you how she feels rather than tell her how

to feel.

☞ Get adult help for problems you don't know how to

handle.

☞

☞

See the Good in "Different"

Going on with life includes accepting that it will never be the same. It also means realizing that life doesn't have to be the same to be good. Every day changes us a little bit. Tomorrow we'll be different than we are today. Both good and bad, big and small experiences make us who we are. The problem with death, disease, accidents, and other sudden pain is the enormity of their impact. We feel like we can't adjust. But we can. God promises to always give us the power: *I can do everything through [Christ] who gives me strength* (Philippians 4:13).

Another problem with death, disease, and accidents is that they just plain hurt. They aren't fair or good or fun. No one will replace Theo's dad or Helena's aunt. There's nothing good about the blindness of Tandy's three-year-old cousin or the stroke that disabled Dan's grandfather. And it's okay to say that. Choosing life doesn't mean we like what has happened. It just means we refuse to let the pain steal the joy.

Why choose life? Because the alternatives are loneliness, boredom, anger, bitterness, and isolation. These synonyms for death highlight the power of life. Suicide is only one way to die—many people kill themselves slowly by cutting themselves off from friends and family, by embracing boredom, by harboring anger (anger is not a sin; refusing to work through the anger is the sin), by nurturing bitterness. Those who refuse life ignore the good God persistently gives.

Choosing life means you have confidence that in the midst of the sadness God cares, cries with you, and works with you to redeem the situation. It means you find and embrace the good. It means you decide to walk on through the pain rather than stop and wallow in it. While you look forward to heaven, you can make the most of your time here on earth. Working side by side with God, you can find, create, and enjoy good.

Even in the midst of the unfairness and the pain, there's something worth living for. There's more to life than pain. There's more than bad circumstances. There's more than death and destruction. Some call it love, others call it faith; but whatever you call it, it's a real and powerful good that cannot be daunted. God is the author of this good. Linking up with God puts you in touch with the good. Caring for family and friends helps you see it in action.

Idealistic? Certainly. But at the same time it's much more realistic than settling for the pain and problems, death and destruction this world has to offer. Love, faith, joy, and serenity are true. They're available. They're real. They're worth it. You can find, contribute to, and live them.

> *And the peace of God, which transcends all understanding, will guard your hearts and your minds in Christ Jesus.*
> *Philippians 4:7*

152

CHAPTER 8

I Won't Forget

MOVE ON AS GRIEF IS RESOLVED AND FORGIVENESS IS ACCEPTED

Isn't it kind of heartless of me to walk, smile, and be happy now that Craig is blind?" Alan asked. "How can I be happy when I'm the one who suggested he try mountain rappelling in the first place? The fall from the mountain stole his sight. It's my fault. Now I can see and he can't. I've asked for and received his forgiveness; he tells me to quit moping around. But I can't forget what happened."

Once we've been through shock, sadness, guilt, regret, anger, depression, and questions and we've decided to go on with life, we must live that decision. Alan's having a rough time doing this. That's okay; it shows he cares. But as he struggles, he must turn his concern into actions that show real love and genuine friendship.

Alan's moping and whining won't help Craig much. Keeping the friendship strong will. As Alan and Craig continue to experience life fully and encourage each other to do so, they live as God intended. Alan must choose to do things with Craig just like before, without letting blindness get in the way. He must learn about Craig's challenges and help him meet them without pity or distance. Pain doesn't have to stop life. We may have to find a way around the pain, but we can still find and enjoy the good God continues to give.

Going on with life after a death or living on with the day-to-day challenges of a disability requires a delicate balance—moving on without forgetting and embracing life without neglecting those who still hurt. It's hard to do, but we can live this balance. We can show in our lives that the person or event made a difference in us but at the same time work around disabilities, diseases, disappointment, and death to find and grasp the good that awaits us. We can refuse to let pain have the victory.

Because Alan has confidence that God cares about Craig's life, and wants him to enjoy life to its fullest, Alan can be instrumental in helping that happen. They can still study together, do sports together, work together, and play together. This is not pity—it's friendship. It's confidence that blindness doesn't have to block life or adventure or goodness.

Craig and Alan still have each other. There are rough times ahead, but they can face them together. A deep and different pain comes when someone dies. Can anyone be happy after something like this happens? If you really care, can you be happy again? Yes. Once you've grieved, you're ready to remember in meaningful ways. You're ready to live your life as a tribute to God and to the special person he placed in your life. You're ready to look forward to reunion in heaven.

How can I be happy when Andrew's dead? He doesn't get to enjoy life. Why should I? I could logically argue that Andrew would want you to enjoy life, that he wouldn't want your life to end because his did. But the feeling remains that it is somehow wrong to go on with life after death or other tragedy. How can you live a full life when someone important is missing? How can you go on without forgetting? How can you remember without dwelling on the past? Balance is the key. Do both: Remember and move on.

Journaling Suggestions

Write your memories of life with your friend or family member. If your friend has been injured or is sick, read or deliver these memoirs to him. He'll feel important, which will speed his healing. [Hint: Even if your friend is unconscious, read or talk to him. Some studies indicate that people can hear even if they can't respond..] If your friend has died, give it to his or her family. Ten-year-old Aaron wrote the memories on page 154 of his three-year-old friend Andrew after an aggressive bacteria stole his life. Both Aaron and Andrew had been battling leukemia.

I remember he liked peanut butter and jelly sandwiches. He almost always brought one along to get him through long waits at the doctor's office. I remember the toy kitten I gave him. I remember the picture of him with that silly grin. I remember him making pizza with imaginary syrup and giving it to me. I remember him coming around the corner—someone always said, "Andrew's here." Then he would say, "We're here!" I remember that he liked my mini-piano, so I gave him one. Then he found out about my real piano and asked me to bring it to him! I remember he had so much to say that he couldn't get it all out. I remember his smile and his love for French fries.

Journaling Suggestions

Consider arranging your memories in an acrostic or other poem form. Use the following acrostic as an example:

Always happy

Never forgot to care

Dear

Really outgoing and observant

Enduring trust

Will always be important in my life

<u>Your acrostic:</u>

Ointment and perfume rejoice the heart: so doth the
sweetness of a man's friend by hearty counsel.

Proverbs 27:9 KJV

Arrange letters, photographs, and mementos of your friend
in a photo album or scrapbook. Smile over the wonderful
times you shared. Cry over the things you miss. Thank God
for the good your friend brought into your life. Share this
notebook with someone who cares about you and your friend.

Write a tribute to the one you miss. Include why you're glad he or she was a part of your life and how you are better because you have known each other. Tell what you most look forward to about being reunited in heaven. Share this tribute with your own family and your friend's family. Consider framing it or keeping it in a special place.

If you made home movies or audio tapes, watch or listen to them. Smile, cry, remember. Look forward to the time you'll be together in heaven (see Revelation 21:4).

If your friend is experiencing a health crisis, has lost an ability (as serious as paralysis or as simple as getting cut from the ball team), or is otherwise going through a rough time, combine some elements of the above suggestions:

1. Write a letter telling what you appreciate about your friend. Include your favorite memories.

2. Create a scrapbook or poster that illustrates why your friend is special to you. Include photos, ticket stubs, or other mementos of times you've shared.

3. Affirm your continuing friendship by telling your hopes for the future.

4. Live out your hopes by continuing to do things together.

If your friend is struggling to overcome an illness or accident, your support and encouragement helps him or her through. Show how much your friend means to you, that you want your friend to join you in living life.

Look beyond your own grief to notice your friend's or family member's feelings about the crisis. Don't assume your friend feels as you do. Alan can ask Craig how he feels about his blindness. He can listen with interest as Craig tells his fears, hopes, dreams, pain, and more. It is hard to find a friend who will listen. Alan can be that friend.

Notice how listening and understanding keeps your friendship alive and growing in the midst of pain.

Some people think it's romantic to not go on after a loved
one has been killed or hurt. Why does this Romeo and
Juliet response cause more pain than it heals? What does
Ephesians 5:15–17 say about this?

How is going on with your life a tribute to your friend or
family member? A tribute to God who gave you to each
other? Draw or doodle your answer.

> How does heaven make your life worth living again? What actions and attitudes will show that your friend or family member made a difference in your life?

Live Your Forgiveness

If you were the cause of your friend's accident or death, or even if you simply regret something you did or didn't do, you may find it extra hard to go on. Conversely, you may have trouble forgiving someone who hurt you. Recognize that it's hard, and then go ahead and live your forgiveness. Because real forgiveness is available, real change can come. Review chapter 3 to discover how to obtain and live forgiveness.

Because you've been forgiven, your life will be different. You can be wiser, more caring, more likely to think ahead. Because you have forgiven others, you can be more sensitive and cooperative. In both cases you'll be more likely to do the loving thing, the action you'll never have to regret. All of us would change things about our past if we could, but since we can't turn back the clock, we must make today and tomorrow the best days they can be. Melanie so wished she'd told her grandfather she loved him one more time. Now she tells people what she appreciates about them the minute she thinks of it. The closeness that grows is a wonderful gift to both Melanie and the people around her.

Learn from your regrets and then free yourself to live on. Alan wasn't the cause of Craig's accident—the climbing equipment had been improperly made. Certainly Craig wouldn't be blind if they hadn't gone mountain rappelling, but accidents can happen anywhere. Neither God nor Alan caused Craig's accident. Craig wishes he weren't blind; Alan wishes Craig weren't blind. But wishes don't make things happen—actions do. While awaiting a medical breakthrough, Craig works on seeing in ways that count: understanding, friendship, giving his best, perceiving the good in people. This is living forgiveness. It's refusing to let the evil steal the good.

No doubt about it, hurting someone intentionally or accidentally produces intense guilt. And so it should: Guilt is designed to keep you from doing wrong. Guilt invites review of the past and a commitment to the future. As we look back, we discover things we could have done better. Craig and Alan could have checked the ropes or had someone else check them. Jennifer could have talked to Ted without losing her temper. Ted could have insisted on seat belts and could have refused the dare. Theo's mom could have worked together with Theo to manage their family grief rather than abandoning him. All five feel sorry, and so they should. But wallowing in guilt keeps them centered on themselves and keeps them from doing the good that will make everyone feel better.

Instead of stopping at guilty, change the way you live. Craig and Alan double-check any equipment they use. Jennifer talks problems through calmly. Ted drives as though his passengers' lives depend on him. Theo and his mom spend time together. Like them, you can talk honestly about your past and ways you want to change. Mistakes, sins, regrets, and forgiveness do little good if they don't change the future.

Journaling Suggestions

Describe or draw what you have done or not done to hurt someone. Why do you feel guilty about it?

Describe or draw how you think God wants your life to be different now that you've been through this wrongdoing.

Psalm 32 documents the way David reviewed his wrong-doing and committed to present and future change. When David ignored his wrong, neither he nor those around him were happy.

> When I kept silent, my bones wasted away through my groaning all day long . . . my strength was sapped as in the heat of summer.

Psalm 32:3–4

Read all of verses 1–4 in your Bible. How is this like your feelings when you hide your wrong or refuse to admit it?

When David confessed his wrong, God cleansed and forgave him. Note this excerpt from Psalm 32:5–7 and then read the complete passage in your Bible.

Then I acknowledged my sin to you and did not cover up my iniquity. I said, "I will confess my transgressions to the LORD"—and you forgave the guilt of my sin.

How does this cleansing feel in your life? How fast does it happen?

The process isn't finished if we stop with forgiveness. We must allow God to show us how to live from here on. Psalm 32:8-11 promises God's specific instruction for amending wrong and for going on with life.

> I [God] will instruct you and teach you in the way you should go; I will counsel you and watch over you. Do not be like the horse or the mule, which have no understanding but must be controlled by bit and bridle.

What action does God want you to take to amend your wrong? To go on with life? To prevent future pain? Why is living a changed life better than going on as though nothing ever happened ("like the horse or the mule")? Why is it better than ignoring past wrongs?

Just saying you'll do better doesn't always work. Sin patterns are persistent. Which of these actions would help you overcome your sin? Choose at least one.

[ ] Invite a friend or family member to keep an eye on you, warning you when he or she sees a sin pattern emerging and complimenting you when you live with love.

[ ] Rewrite the event as you wish it had happened. Live that new story.

[ ] Practice conversations and encounters ahead of time.

[ ] Take time to feel bad. Feeling sorry about the past can keep you from repeating the same mistakes in the future.

[ ] Refuse to continue to feel bad. Rather than let the past doom the future, let it make a positive difference. Let past wrongs bring future right. Because you cannot change the past, work hard on the present.

Decide what opposite-to-the-past actions you will take.

For example, be honest in relationships rather than hide

your feelings; deliberately use your words to encourage

rather than humiliate; act safely rather than recklessly;

take time for people rather than rush. See Colossians 3 for

some opposite-to-sin actions to try.

[ ] Before acting or speaking, consider how you would feel

if someone treated you that way.

[ ]

Illustrate how you'll do the one (or more) you chose.

WILL I EVER FEEL GOOD AGAIN?

Understand People's Reactions

Even when you can move on with life, others might not want you to. Heather was driving the car when her friend Tami was killed. Every time she goes down a certain hall at school, the group that gathers there whispers, "There goes the girl who killed Tami." Others are more direct with their comments: "You've got your *nerve* going to parties and having fun when Tami's dead. Don't you care?"

The comments sting Heather every time she hears them, but she's learned to respond rather than react. She recognizes that the hall group misses Tami too. Their comments are an attempt to blame someone, as though blaming would bring Tami back. Rather than snap back, Heather recognizes their comments as misdirected grief. She responds with, "Of course I care. Nobody wishes Tami were alive more than I do. If my withdrawing from life would bring Tami back, I'd do it in a minute."

To some people who understand she says, "I don't feel like going on, but I do because two people dying would be a double loss. Maybe I can do some of the good Tami would have done."

Heather's pain is doubly deep because she is responsible for her friend's death. Even when the tragedy is not directly connected to you, you wonder what you might have done to prevent it. Perhaps you wish you'd done or not done a specific something before the tragedy.

Like Heather, you agonize over the people you lose by death, the pain your friends go through, the adjustments they must make, the changes you must choose. Walk through your pain by writing or drawing your responses to the following ideas. Invite God to walk with you. Experience his power and healing.

Journaling Suggestions

Write one or more comments people have said about a loss you've endured or a mistake you made. Was it helpful or hurtful? Suggest a reason for the comment and an answer God wants you to make. When is no answer at all the best choice?

<u>Comment</u>

If you cared you wouldn't be so happy.

<u>Reason for the comment</u>

Anger that you're okay and someone else is not.

<u>Redemptive response</u>

I'd bring her back if I could, but I can't. I'm trying to do some of the good she can no longer do.

A gentle answer turns away wrath, but a harsh word stirs up anger.

Proverbs 15:1

Draw or describe what you want people to say or do for you to help you go on with life.

Who might be willing to treat you this way? Let him or her know what you need. Jot how you will ask for this treatment.

Draw or describe what you don't want people to say or do.

Experiencing other people's helpful and not-so-helpful comments helps you know how to be a genuine help rather than an obstacle in someone's path. How will you treat friends who are trying to go on after pain? See Colossians 3:5-14 for ideas.

Therefore, as God's chosen people, holy and dearly loved, clothe yourselves with compassion, kindness, humility, gentleness and patience.

Colossians 3:8, 12

Show Confidence in the Future

Ultimately, moving on means you know the present pain won't last forever. You're going to make it through the rough times to the perfection that awaits in heaven. Craig will get his sight back in heaven. Melanie will be reunited with her grandfather there. Kelly will walk, dance, and skip again. Jerry can stop fighting against cancer. Theo will find more friends who care, both now and forever. While you wait, determine to find and enjoy the good God continues to give. Nothing on this earth is permanent or safe—the earth's imperfections bring sickness, tragedy, and pain. God doesn't like it and he will change it. One day all tears, death, sorrow, and pain will pass away (Revelation 21:4). One day we'll treat each other with love, we'll enjoy each other's presence without good-byes, and we'll live in complete security. This is the essence of hope: having confidence that there are better days ahead and living in light of that confidence. If things were going to stay this bad, we might as well just give up. But they won't.

172

Because we have a bright future and a God who cares, we can focus on the good and make it through the pain. As 1 Thessalonians 4:13 explains, we don't have to grieve like those who have no hope. We can grieve with hope. In the midst of our pain, we can live the love, find the enjoyment, and savor the security of God right here and right now.

And God shall wipe away all tears from their eyes; and there shall be no more death, neither sorrow, nor crying, neither shall there be any more pain: for the former things are passed away.

Revelation 21:4 KJV

Journaling Suggestions

Recall that grief comes in waves and that some of those waves overlap or come together. Over the next several weeks, keep a journal of the shock, sadness, guilt, anger, depression, and questions that come your way. Note also the times when you feel good, confident about life, and certain that God can and will meet your every need (see Philippians 4:19). Thank God for staying with you through it all.

CHAPTER 9

Giver's Guide

TIPS FOR MINISTERING
TO GRIEVING FRIENDS

When tragedy strikes a friend, we feel helpless. We stand by as grief and guilt grip and twist them. We yearn to take their pain away. We cannot remove their pain, ease their guilt, or go through grief for them, but we can guide them through it safely. We can love them, walk beside them, listen, and offer resources. The book in your hand is one of these resources.

When sad things happen, both the people in crises and those around them go through grief and guilt. They grieve for what they've lost. They feel guilty for what they did or didn't do before the tragedy, what they might have done to prevent it, or what they did to cause it. They feel angry about what has happened and wonder why it happened at all. Too often friends suffer these heavyweight emotions alone because the people around them don't notice, because they urge them to "hurry up and get over it," or because Christians equate sadness with lack of faith. Too often we applaud those who go through tragedy without a tear. Then we wonder why people act strangely. We wonder why they hide their feelings.

Young people grieve over much more than death. They grieve when a friend moves away. They grieve over leaving one school to start another. They grieve when parents divorce or when they or a friend encounter a serious disease. They grieve when they make a mistake or hurt a friend. The more serious the change, the deeper and longer lasting the grief.

You can help your friend through the dark days by accepting his sad feelings and encouraging him to express them to God. Even if the tragedy happened a long time ago, your friend may have ignored the pain and left it unhealed. Journaling suggestions like the ones in this book offer opportunities to explore sadness and find God's healing for current, past, or anticipated pain.

Remember that grief comes in stages. Though the stages are predictable, the time a person spends in each stage is not. We do know that it usually takes about a year to recover from a significant loss such as the death of a grandparent or the discovery of a handicap. We also know that grief is cyclical and wavelike, recurring and surging at holidays, significant times of the year, or during certain shared experiences. Give your friends the time they need to grieve while gently urging them to move on with life. Guide them to grieve with health, with hope, and with love.

Because the stages are seldom clearly defined, the following actions provide H.E.L.P.S. all along the way.

Help, don't do it. As much as you want to, you can't walk through grief for your friend. She needs your support as she walks through grief, but there is much of it she must do herself. Only she can feel the pain. Only she can recall the memories. Only she can move through pain to the joy on the other side. Only she can invite God along on all these steps. You can sit with her and hug her when she's sad. You can listen as she recounts memories and add your memories. You can continue to be there through the darkest days. You can pray that your friend will recognize and bask in God's steady love and provision. Perhaps Galatians 6:2, 5 best illustrates the twofold nature of grief:

Carry each other's burdens, and in this way you will fulfill the law of Christ . . . for each one should carry his own load.

E*quip them with information.* Grief emotions are powerful, frightening, and confusing. Assure your friend that it's okay to be both sad and mad, that there is a path out of guilt and regret, that it's okay to ask questions. Let your friend know that he is not crazy when he dreams about his dead loved one or when he thinks he sees him at the mall. Confirm that grief can take a long time. Explain the stages of grief and emphasize its healing importance. Point out that your friend can move on with life comfortable with the uneasy mix of continuing grief and normal routine.

L*et them grieve in their way and at their pace.* Don't believe you know how your friend feels until she *tells* you how she feels. Don't insist that your friend cry or refuse to cry. Don't push talking if your friend prefers quiet. Rather than hurry or slow the grief process, trust your friend to take the time she needs. Grief is personal. Though the general experiences are the same, each person grieves in his or her own way. Let your friend tell you his feelings and needs rather than prescribing to him what to do and feel.

P*rovide physical affection in the form that is most comfortable to your friend.* Human touch conveys the security and love grieving people need. Some people like hugs, others prefer smiles, a pat on the shoulder, a squeeze of the elbow. Some people want to be hugged privately, others don't mind if a crowd is around. A touch on the elbow or a hug around the shoulders can communicate more than words ever could.

See you and God as a team. Work alongside God. Don't try to replace him. Let God heal your friend with his steady love. Assure your friend of God's constant presence and care, point your friend to Bible promises, and pray steadily for your friend.

Love Stage by Stage

As you understand and observe your friend passing through the stages of grief, take action to care. Let these examples spur you to discover actions that help the friends you care for.

Shock

Your friend can hardly think about or believe the sad event. She's numb and has trouble feeling anything. Think of shock as emotional overload. This usually takes place the first day through the first week. See chapter 1 for an exploration of shock.

Don't	Do
Try to talk your friend into reality.	Hug, hold, love, stay close.
Ask your friend to snap out of it.	Compose a letter or tape telling your friend why he is valuable to you.
Assume your friend is not facing reality.	Agree that this sad event is hard to believe.

Sadness

Crying, sobbing, sighing, despair, and loneliness can occur anytime. These emotions express the deep sadness your friend feels. God can use these emotions to cleanse and heal. See chapter 2 for information that can help your friend move through sadness.

<u>Don't</u>	<u>Do</u>
Say "Don't cry."	Say, "I'm glad you trust me enough to cry with me."
Push your friend to cry.	Let him express the sadness he feels in the way that is healthiest for him.
Try to schedule emotion.	Let your friend feel the emotions at his pace and timing.

Guilt

Guilt frequently accompanies grief. Your friend may feel responsible for the accident or illness. She may actually be responsible for what happened. She may feel guilty for doing or not doing something with or for the one who died. She may regret a fight they had or cruel words she said. She may wish she'd witnessed more vigorously to an unsaved friend. Some of these guilt feelings will be true guilt, others not. But all guilt feelings are important. Your friend needs genuine forgiveness for genuine guilt and the ability to accept and live that forgiveness. She also needs to rename false guilt as regret and find freedom to move past it. Care for your friend by listening to her feelings of guilt, whether real or imagined. See chapter 3 for ideas.

<u>Don't</u>	<u>Do</u>
Say "It's okay, you didn't do anything wrong."	Help your friend explore what happened to separate real guilt from false.

Don't	Do
Assume all guilt is false guilt.	Hear your friend's confessions (see James 5:16).
Dismiss false guilt.	Help your friend rename it as regret. Suggest actions like writing a letter to the deceased or saying how he wishes things had gone. See chapter 3 for more ideas on moving past guilt and regret.
Assume your friend feels forgiven.	Guide your friend to accept and live God's forgiveness day by day.
Say "This was God's will."	Notice that people have choices and many of those choices don't please God. Agree that God hates evil and injustice even more than we do. See chapter 6 for more on God's will.
Insist your friend tell you everything.	Encourage your friend to talk primarily with God.
Dismiss real guilt.	Guide your friend to confess, find forgiveness, and make resitution where possible.

Anger

Your friend may feel angry at the situation, at the doctors, at God, at himself, even at the person who died or became sick. Assure your friend that anger means pain and that God wants to heal this pain. Rather than fear anger, free your friend to be angry but not sin (see Ephesians 4:26). As your friend walks through anger, feels it, thinks and prays through it, he will discover what God wants him to do about it. Because anger is such a sensitive emotion, your friend may need extra help with this stage of grief. See chapter 4 for guidelines on walking through anger.

Don't	Do
Call anger a sin.	Encourage your friend to walk through his anger without hurting someone.
Fear anger.	Hear your friend's feelings, confident of God's healing power.
Discourage anger at God.	Remind your friend that God can handle his anger and wants to heal it. Then guide your friend to point the anger at the real cause.
Accept any angry action.	Help your friend let her anger out in healing ways, searching Scripture and chapter 4 for ideas.

Depression

Commonly occurring a week or two after the funeral and at significant times like birthdays and Christmas, depression makes your friend wonder if she can go on without her loved one. She may feel desperately lonely and very vulnerable. Hear her sadness and assure her that she can make it. See chapters 5 and 7 for actions that help us move through the dark days to the light on the other side.

Don't	Do
Avoid your friend when she's sad.	Spend time with her to show she has friends who care.
Pepper your friend with Bible verses.	Live the Bible in your caring actions. Your continuing love and interest assures her that God is with her and cares.
Choose Bible verses about rejoicing during sadness.	Choose Bible verses that show God's involvement during sadness, such as Philippians 4:19 and Psalm 23.
Assume you know how your friend feels.	Invite your friend to tell you how she feels.

182

Questions

Your friend may wonder why the sad thing has happened to him. He may fear that God is mad at him or that he has done something for which he's being punished. Assure him that both good and bad happen to everyone in this imperfect world, and that suffering makes God as sad as it does us. Explain that God offers his power for getting through the sad time. He's the source of good, not the giver of bad. See chapter 7 for a more thorough exploration of this difficult "why" question.

Don't	Do
Imply that God likes or gives bad circumstances.	Explain that God allows evil for the sake of a greater good, but that he does not like evil in any way.

Don't	Do
Give pat answers.	Encourage your friend to share the answers he's found. Then talk over the strengths and weaknesses in each.
Insist on a firmly worked out answer.	Assure your friend that God is the answer, not an explanation about God.

Acceptance

With time, your friend will begin to feel like herself again. Note two important truths about acceptance. First, acceptance does not mean it's all over. Birthdays, doctor check-ups, and other events will bring waves of fresh grief. Second, the only way to get to acceptance is to go through the shock, sadness, guilt, forgiveness, anger, and other forms of grief. There is no shortcut. See chapter 8 for actions that bring healthy acceptance.

Don't	Do
Assume it's all over.	Notice tough times, remember milestones, listen with sensitivity.
Forget.	Write anniversaries, holidays, and doctor appointments on your calendar, and send notes or care in other ways.
Minimize the suffering because your friend has decided to go on.	Agree that it's hard.

Don't	**Do**
Stop mentioning the person, event, or disability.	Ask, share memories; balance tribute with talking about other parts of life.
Make heroes of grieving people who move on with life.	Recognize how hard it is to move on. Privately commend your friend for other things he does well.

Rejoice with those who rejoice; mourn with those who mourn.

Romans 12:15

CHAPTER 10

Leader's Guide

EXPLORE GRIEF IN A GROUP

Let the ideas in this section guide your group to walk through their sadness safely. Because not all students are currently grieving, this study can also prepare students for future grief or heal them from past unresolved grief. Notice also how studying together builds the kind of caring group in which members help one another through sad times.

Ideally each student should have a copy of *Will I Ever Feel Good Again?* to read at home and write in during class. As God and you guide this study, feel free to adapt these procedures to meet the unique needs of your group members. The procedures suggest participatory learning because students learn better when they seek and find the answers themselves.

Most students find it extremely difficult to talk about sadness, death, and grief. They show this anxiety with giggles, morbid jokes, wild behavior, and more. This guide eases them into sharing by moving from easy-to-talk-about questions to more difficult, soul-searching ones. Each session begins with an active fact-finding activity and then moves toward personal evaluation and growth.

As you teach, ask God to work alongside you to create a caring group. This is perhaps even more important than the content you teach. As your group develops the kind of love and mutual support that makes healing possible, students will walk through their grief with faith and strength.

Session 1 (overview of grief, focus on chapter 1)

1. To introduce the topic of grief, overview the book, and guide students to overcome popular misconceptions about grief, post one sign on each of the four walls of the room:

AGREE   DISAGREE   STRONGLY AGREE   STRONGLY DISAGREE

Instruct students to stand in the center of the room. Explain that when you read a statement, students are to move to the sign that describes how they feel about it. Read each of the following statements one at a time, repeating until each student has moved to a sign. After each statement, invite one or more from each group to tell why they chose as they did. Begin with the smallest group to reward their courage to stand with a minority. Encourage healthy interaction and learning from one another. Note that each statement is multifaceted—it has many sides that are true—so one can disagree and still bring out some truth about grief. Supplement the discussion with the comments and chapters in parentheses.

❖ *When death or some other bad experience happens, it's best to just not think about it.* (To go on with life we must take some time to be sad and to remember. This helps God heal us. If we don't grieve, the sadness remains under the surface and comes out in unhealthy or destructive ways. Ecclesiastes 3:1, 4 explains that we must take time to grieve.)

❖ *When people don't cry at a funeral, it means they are taking it well.* (They are likely in shock. This is a time when reality hasn't hit, a time of emotional overload that prepares them for the rough time ahead. In addition, some people don't cry to express sadness. Comment from chapter 1.)

❖ *Grief is over in the first two weeks.* (The feelings of shock often end in that time, but grieving over death, a serious disease, or a disability may take a year or more and recur during holidays or other significant times. After a funeral we need friends and family more than ever.)

❖ *Christians shouldn't grieve, because their loved ones are in heaven.* (It is true that loved ones are happy, but we miss them. So we need to grieve. First Thessalonians 4:13 advises us to grieve but to do so with hope. Ask: What is our hope? Jesus is coming back to take us to live with him forever.)

❖ *Grief comes in a predictable pattern.* (Shock, sadness, guilt, anger, depression, and acceptance are parts of grief, but they don't always come in the same pattern. Comment from chapter 1.)

❖ *Nobody can ever replace a person who dies.* (True. No one takes anyone else's place, but God will meet your needs through other people. Comment from chapter 2.)

187

❖ *There are some things we can never forgive ourselves for.* (Some actions are truly terrible, but refusing to forgive ourselves helps no one. After receiving God's forgiveness and forgiving ourselves, we can do good. Rather than ignore the past or immobilize ourselves we can balance regret with going on, mourn over the wrong, redeem the past as best we can, learn from past mistakes, and keep from making future ones. Comment from chapter 3).

❖ *Being angry at God is sin.* (God can handle our anger—anger usually means pain, and God can heal our pain when we tell him about our anger. Letting anger keep us separated from God is sin because it cuts us off from the source of support and strength. The best way to respond to a friend's anger is to listen and to agree that it hurts. Comment from chapter 4.)

❖ *Feeling like you can't go on means you probably can't.*
(This feeling is a sign of sadness or depression, not a signal
to end it all. Keep walking, confident that God will give you
power to make it through the dark days. See Isaiah 40:30–31
and comment from chapter 5.)

❖ *It's wrong to question God.* (Questioning God shows we
trust him to have the answers. It becomes wrong only when
we refuse to listen to God's answers or to trust God as The
Answer. Comment from chapter 6.)

❖ *Sometimes there's nothing you can do to get over a loss.*
(It may be hard, but God always provides pathways to happiness. We can always decide to find joy. We can make it
until heaven comes. Comment from chapter 7.)

❖ *Going on means you've forgotten about the sad event.*
(No, it means you're ready to move on and are comfortable with memories. We can balance life with death, hope
with sadness, regret with change. Comment from chapter 8.)

188

2. Ask: What's your first reaction to talking about
death or other sad experiences? (Examples: avoid talking or thinking about it; think if we ignore sadness it
might go away; would rather talk about happiness.) Agree
that sadness is not easy to talk about, but talking about
it can heal us and deepen our confidence in God. Suggest
that focusing on death or other sad experiences for con-
centrated periods can give us life in the fullest sense.
"Grief" is the fancy name for this. Through grief we discover that sadness hurts tremendously but that the pain
won't last. Because of Jesus' resurrection, we can experience life after death, both here on earth and later in
heaven.

3. Explain grief by directing students to write G.R.I.E.F.
vertically on the inside back cover of their books. Guide
them to make an acrostic by providing these principles.

Go back over the life of the one who died.

Remember what you liked and didn't like, what you did and wish you had done.

I hurt—admit it and talk to God about it.

Energy—you'll be low on energy for a while. That's okay.

Find a friend to talk to. We all need each other to make it through the tough times. Be this friend for others going through grief.

Ask: What experience do we usually associate with grief? (Death.) Point out that any sad experience invites at least a few minutes of grief. Direct each student to name a different experience that would cause grief, scanning "Choose the Path That Leads Back to Happiness" in chapter 1 for ideas.

Ask: Why can't we just brush sadness aside? Why do we need to take time to grieve? Encourage students to skim chapter 1 for ideas. Explain that grieving—reviewing the sad event, feeling the emotions, and deciding what to do next—leads to healing. If we don't feel the sadness, it comes out in destructive ways and we never heal. Walking through the pain leads us to the good we yearn for. Invite a volunteer to read Ecclesiastes 3:1, 4.

4. Point out that grief comes in waves, sometimes called stages. Supply blue paper to simulate waves. Direct six students or six teams of students to explain each wave/stage as described under "Ride the Waves" in chapter 1. They may make their explanation in skit, advertisement, or speech form but must use the blue paper in some way. As part of their explanation, invite them to name a way they have experienced or think they would experience this wave of grief. After each explanation, invite others to add how they have experienced this wave. Review the five truths about waves (come in types and in stages; not always in order; two or

more may come together; all can be ridden safely; wave may come back again).

5. Focus on shock as the first wave. Comment briefly from the beginning of chapter 1. Invite students to complete the first section of journaling suggestions in chapter 1 and then to share with the group how they have experienced shock. Ask: How have people helped you through shock? Hurt you? How do you think shock gets you ready for the journey through grief? What ways do you want to be cared for and care for others during shock? Why is going through sadness the only way back to joy—why can't we just avoid sad feelings?

6. Ask: Why is grief more like a tunnel than a wall? What would be wrong with seeing sad events as a wall? (We'd see no way out.) Guide students to complete the tunnel journaling activity in chapter 1 and to share their recordings. Point out: Grief is like riding the waves and is like a tunnel. Ask: What else is grief like? Not like?

7. Explain that the Bible encourages us to take a friend along on our grief journey. Invite a student to read Psalm 23:4 and complete the associated journaling activity in chapter 1. Ask: Who is the friend who can always accompany us, the friend described in this verse? (God.) Ask: How has, or could, God help you through death or other sadness? Explain: Frequently God loves us through people. Invite students to tell about how a family member or friend has helped through a sad experience.

Music option: Emphasize that we need other people to help us through sad times. We can be those people for each other. Play a support song such as "Everybody Needs a Little Help" by David Meece (from *Everybody Needs a Little Help:* Myrrh, 1978) with the words displayed. Encourage students to sing along and tell how the song applies to their lives.

Session 2 (chapters 2 and 5)

1. As students enter give each a lump of clay. Direct them to shape it into sadness. Point out the descriptions of sadness in the beginning of chapter 2 for ideas. Call for each to explain their sculptures. Use their sculptures to bring out points from chapters 2 and 5. Recall that we studied shock in the first session and we'll address sadness and depression during this session.

2. Invite each student to describe a sadness they've felt using the three-letter form in the journaling section on page 26. Explain that sadness comes after the shock wears off and that a deeper sadness called depression often occurs a few days or weeks later. Ask: What's the difference between sadness and depression? Assure students that though depression tends to be longer and deeper, both are healed with similar actions. Depression just takes longer.

3. Distribute paper plates and direct students to draw a face on the outside that shows how they look on the outside when they are sad, and to cover the inside of the plate with how they look on the inside when they are sad. Invite each student to show the plate. Ask: How do we experience sadness similarly? Differently? Is it okay for Christians to be sad? (YES!) Recall that when Jesus felt sadness in John 11:35, people saw it as a sign of love for Lazarus. How does experiencing sadness help us heal? How does experiencing sadness make it possible to help others through sadness, even when they are sad about something different? Call on a volunteer to read 2 Corinthians 1:3–5.

4. Direct students to write a passage of sorrow similar to Lamentations 3:16–25 as guided by chapter 2. Ask: How does sadness impact your need to write or express your feelings? How do you express your sadness? Do you feel more or less creative when you're sad?

5. Ask: According to chapter 2, what three H actions help us through sadness? (Hold, hide, heal.) How have one or

more of these helped you through a sad or depressed time? What other H action might help? What is hope? What does it look like? Feel like? How does it get us through sadness? What's the difference between sadness with and without hope? Direct students to reshape their sadness clay to show hope in the midst of sadness. Explain that the Bible promises real hope for real sadness. Point out the sample Bible promises in chapter 2. Ask: Which is your favorite? What others do you personally depend on?

Focus on Bible passages of hope by playing hangman. Write the Bible promise references on the chalkboard to help students guess. If your group is small, let students play individually; if larger, play by teams. Write dashes on the chalkboard to match each letter of the phrase (NIV translation unless otherwise noted—feel free to change to students' favorite translation). For example "Weeping may linger for the night" would be written:

- - - - - - -   - - -   - - - - - -   - - -   - - -   - - - - -

Invite the first individual or team to name a consonant (any letter but A, E, I, O, or U). If the letter is in the phrase, fill it in and give the group a card representing 100 points for each time it appears. Groups may guess vowels by turning in two cards (200 points) and may guess the phrase once with each successful letter. Remind group members to keep their Bibles open to the passages. After each phrase is guessed, ask: How would this truth get you through a sad time? Bible references and suggested phrases:

Psalm 30:5 (NRSV)   Weeping may linger for the night
                           Joy comes with the morning

Lamentations 3:22–25   Because of the Lord's great love
                               we are not consumed
                           For his compassions never fail

	They are new every morning
	Great is your faithfulness
	The Lord is my portion; therefore I will wait for him
	The Lord is good to those whose hope is in him
Philippians 1:6 (NRSV)	The one who began a good work among you will bring it to completion
Psalm 23:4	Though I walk through the valley of the shadow of death, I will fear no evil
	For you are with me
	Your rod and your staff, they comfort me
John 14:1–3	Do not let your hearts be troubled
	Trust in God; trust also in me
	In my Father's house are many rooms
	I go and prepare a place for you
	I will come back and take you to be with me
1 Thess. 4:13–14, 17	We do not want you to be ignorant
	Or to grieve like the rest of men, who have no hope
	Jesus died and rose again
	So we believe that God will bring with Jesus those who have fallen asleep in him
	Will be caught up with them in the clouds to meet the Lord
	And so we will be with the Lord forever

Hebrews 4:15–16   For we do not have a high priest
who is unable to sympathize
We have one who has been
tempted in every way, just as
we are
Let us then approach the throne
of grace with confidence
We may receive mercy and find
grace to help us in our time of
need

6. Turn students' focus to chapter 5, which addresses the deeper sadness we call depression. Point out that depression often comes after the waves of shock, sadness, guilt, and anger, but we'll address it here because it is most closely related to sadness. Direct students to complete and share the first series of journaling suggestions in chapter 5.

7. Ask: How do you know God is with you even when you can't feel him? Invite students to share their favorite passage of presence, drawing on the examples in chapter 5. Ask: This chapter describes God as "constant." What other single word would you use to describe him when you are depressed? Call on a volunteer to read Isaiah 40:31. Ask: What's good about each type of going on during sadness: soaring? running? walking?

8. Invite students to remember the last time they felt depressed and to write a song, poem, or prayer about it, using the space provided in chapter 5. Invite volunteers to share what they wrote. Ask: How does writing about or otherwise expressing our sadness equip us to go on?

Call on a volunteer to read Deuteronomy 30:19–20. Why is going on to find and live the joy better than stopping? Invite students to write a story about themselves going on in the midst of deep sadness. As they share their stories ask: Why do we do things more slowly when we're going through a sad time? Why is this okay? How do retreats help us continue with life while we heal? Why is going on during depression better than taking depression out on others? Better than suicide?

9. Direct trios of students to write prescriptions for preventing suicide. Suggest they use the "Refuse Suicide" section in chapter 5 for ideas. As they share their ideas ask: How can we be the types of friends who help each other want to live? How can we prevent the despair that leads to suicide? How can we help people in our school choose life rather than death? Suggest listening, genuine interest, and expressed care as great places to start.

10. Agree that it's easier to talk about choosing life than to do it. Ask: What tools will you use to actually choose life? Pray that we'll all draw on God's power to live life.

Session 3 (chapters 3 and 4)

1. Recall that grief means traveling through a sad experience to the joy on the other side, that grief takes time, and that only by traveling through grief can we find happiness again. Help students recall the six waves of grief by dividing paper into six equal sections, labeling them SHOCK, SADNESS, GUILT, ANGER, DEPRESSION, and ACCEPTANCE, duplicating a set for each student, and cutting them apart. When students arrive, count out a set for each student, shuffle them, and give students six cards that do not form a set. Direct students to trade the cards one at a time until they have a set of six. This process helps students memorize the six stages/waves of grief. Call on volunteers to recite the six waves without looking at their cards. Then invite them to put the waves in the order they typically come (as above). Recall that waves don't always come in order, can overlap, and can repeat. Finally, invite students to tell how they have experienced one of the waves.

Recall that we studied shock in the first session, sadness and depression in the second session; we'll address guilt and anger during this session.

2. Ask: Are there any feelings that are wrong to feel? If so, what? Point out that guilt and anger are two feelings many people condemn or avoid. Hasten to explain that no feeling is bad and that all feelings can lead to good. Ask: How can guilt lead to good? How can anger lead to good? Supplement with chapters 3 and 4. Point out that the actions that follow guilt and anger can be bad, but the feelings are not.

3. Direct students' attention to the stories at the beginning of chapter 3. Ask: How will each feel guilty for what happened? Why? How is guilt a kind of sadness? What have you felt guilty about and what have you done about it?

Guide students to draw, in the space provided in chapter 3, a cartoon about how they wish they could change the circumstances surrounding something sad that happened to them. Invite the group to suggest actions to redo or make the most of each regret.

Ask: What is the difference between guilt and regret? How do we treat them differently? The same? Encourage students to glean their ideas from the Bible and chapter 3. Encourage them to worry less about distinguishing guilt and regret than about healing them. Ask: What are two dangerous extremes for dealing with guilt and regret? (Ignore and immobilize; see "Avoid the Extremes" in chapter 3.) What balance is better, and why? Invite the group to share experiences demonstrating the danger of the extremes and the health of the balance. Share briefly from your own life.

4. Direct students to turn to 1 John 1:8–9 in their Bibles and ask for a volunteer to read it. Ask: What two things does God do when we confess? How does this passage apply to your guilt? Point out that we don't just confess, we let God purify us and guide us to do right next time. Guide students to walk through the 1 John 1:8–9 confession and cleansing process provided in the chapter 3 journal space.

Sensitively guide students to pair with a friend they trust (or to stay in the group if your group is small) and to confess a sin they want forgiveness for. This can be different from the one they wrote about. Guide the group to forgive each student who confesses. Point out that God is the only one who can actually forgive sin, but as we hear confessions, we act as priests to one another and help each other feel forgiven (see 1 Peter 2:9). Motivate deep sensitivity and caring. Skip this group confession if your group will not provide care.

Ask: Why is it hard to accept God's forgiveness? What actions and truths will help us live as forgiven people? Why must repentance come with forgiveness? What lifestyle changes show we truly regret what we have done? How can we keep forgiveness from becoming cheap or trivial? How can forgiveness lead us to avoid causing future pain? Assure students that redeeming the past is not easy. Satan will continue to torment us with the past and try to convince us there is no hope. Encourage students to deliberately turn away from Satan's lies and turn to people who help them live the truth.

5. Show students how to review, rethink, and decide what's next using the exercises in chapter 3. Invite each student to choose a different "decide what's next" action and give an example of when it would be necessary.

6. Invite a volunteer to read Deuteronomy 30:19–20. Guide students to write and sign a commitment to value people, life, joy, the present, and the future. These can be individual commitments or written as a group. In both cases, direct students to use specific examples and to witness each other's signatures with their own. Ask: How do these actions choose life?

7. Ask: Is it okay to be mad about sad events? Why? Supplement from the opening section of chapter 4. Ask: How does God share your anger? Your pain? Discover a true picture of God rather than rumors about God.

8. Emphasize anger as a good gift from God that warns of something wrong, either within or without. This something wrong needs attention. Guide students to complete the "See Things Clearly" suggestions in chapter 4. Ask: How do

you know God cares about you? What animal or animal combination is your anger like? What pain does your most recent anger indicate?

9. Demonstrate how to put anger where it belongs, think it through, and adjust the vent using the journaling suggestions in these chapter 4 sections. Ask: Who do you blame most often when you're angry? Is this the right source? How easy do you find it to think straight when you're angry? What sentences and words do you use to think through anger? What gives anger a bad reputation? How can we change that reputation? Do you tend to let your anger out too fast or too slowly? How will you adjust your vent? Burn off your excess anger?

10. As youth decide what to do about their anger, divide students into teams and challenge them to race to find the most ways to heal anger in Ephesians 4:25–32 and other Bible verses of their choice. Provide paper. Ask: How does God guide you to express your anger? Explore the rest of the "Decide What to Do about Your Anger" section by inviting each youth to choose an action he/she thinks would work best to heal his/her current anger and to tell why. Who helps you feel and manage your anger? Why do abuse and holding anger in fail to work? What do you think God wants you to do about your anger?

Guide students to compose a song or rhyme that helps them remember the four anger managers (put anger where it belongs, think it through, adjust the vent, decide what to do about it) plus any others they suggest.

Session 4 (chapters 6 through 8)

1. Review the Bible passages studied in the past three sessions and those to be studied in this fourth session with a drawing game. Before students arrive, write these passage references on the chalkboard and write phrases from them on individual cards: Session 1—Ecclesiastes 3:1, 4 (sample phrases: there is a time for everything; a season for every activity under heaven;

a time to weep; a time to laugh; a time to mourn; a time to dance); Psalm 23:4. Session 2—John 11:35; 2 Corinthians 1:3–5; Isaiah 40:31. Session 3—1 John 1:9; Deuteronomy 30:19–20; Ephesians 4:25–32. Session 4—James 1:13, 16–17; Ephesians 2:14, 22; John 14:27; 1 Peter 4:12, 19; 2 Corinthians 1:3–5; Psalm 32; Proverbs 15:1; Revelation 21:4.

Direct students to form teams of about four and give each team a stack of paper and a pencil. Explain that the Bible is the best place for advice on how to make it through sadness and how to help our friends do so. Give the following directions: "We'll examine some of these passages through this learning game. Each team will send me a member and I'll show you a phrase from the Bible. When I say go, return to your team and draw the phrase. The first team to guess wins that round. Your team may refer to the Bible. The Scripture passages are displayed on the chalkboard."

After each phrase is guessed, invite students to tell how it helps them through a sad time. Point out that by guessing the phrases, they have settled valuable helping actions in their minds.

2. Distribute paper and direct students to write their first reaction to these questions: Why do sad things happen? Why do sad things happen to good people? Why do we have to die? Invite students to share what they wrote. Explain that these questions have troubled Christians for centuries and that even when we can't find complete answers, we can find satisfying answers.

Direct students to open to chapter 6. Ask: Why does Jerry think he got sick? What's wrong with his answer? What images do people have of God that don't match the way God is? Encourage students to draw a picture of God as he really is in the space provided. Ask: How do you know God is like this? Encourage students to match their pictures with the Bible.

3. Ask: Why do you think God allows pain? Encourage students to refer to "Ask Your Questions" and "Keep Asking until You Understand" for ideas. Guide students to complete the journaling suggestions in these sections and to share their insights. Assure students that God does not give evil, that he hurts when we hurt, and that he is on our side. Ask: How do we know God's not out to get us? What questions do you have for God? Why is it good to ask God our questions? How do the three tips for dealing with hard questions in chapter 6 help? What Bible promises or other actions help you answer your hard questions? Motivate the group to suggest verses and answers for each other.

4. Ask: What pat answers under "Evaluate What You Hear" have you heard? Which have you used? Guide students to dramatize a dialogue between themselves and someone who answered them with a pat answer. Ask: What words would be better? Direct students to redo the skit and to write these better words in their books next to the pat words they replace. Explain that it's usually best to let a friend tell how he sees God rather than give your view.

In addition to replacing the pat phrases in their books, guide students to come up with a helping guide of dos and don'ts such as these based on Bible verses. Students don't have to name a verse with each idea, but encourage them to do so when they know one.

<u>Do</u>	<u>Don't</u>
Encourage one another with true words. (1 Thessalonians 4:18)	Use clichés that sound good but hurt.
Weep with those who weep. (Romans 12:15)	Make fun of tears.
Carry one another's burdens. (Galatians 6:2)	Assume your friend can handle it alone.

Do	**Don't**
Sympathize. (Hebrews 4:15)	Assume it's not your problem.
Be quick to listen, slow to speak. (James 1:19)	Do all the talking.
Confess your sins to each other. (James 5:16)	See your friend as a bum if he confesses a wrongdoing.

5. Ask: Why is God himself, not answers about him, the answer you need? Guide students to complete the final journaling suggestion in chapter 6 as a testimony to this. Invite volunteers to read Ephesians 2:14, 22 and John 14:27 with excitement and enthusiasm, as though they've just discovered these truths. Guide students to memorize these verses by setting them to music: Enlist a volunteer to start a rhythm or rap and the group to say the verses to the rhythm.

6. Point out that the shock, sadness, guilt, anger, depression, and questions can make us feel like it's just not worth going on. Invite students to share a time they found it tough to go on (maybe now). Ask: What gave, or could give you, the motivation to go on? How was your experience like Theo's story in chapter 7? Assure students that God always provides doors to happiness. Ask: How have you seen this in your life?

Direct students to mime actions people have done to show them love in hard times. As the group guesses the actions being mimed, suggest students doodle the actions on page 132 of chapter 7. Ask: How are these people's actions gifts from God?

7. Write the word D-E-C-I-S-I-O-N, one letter to a card, and give one card to each student in scrambled order. If you have more than eight students, make multiple sets and divide students into teams. Challenge students to unscramble the

letters to form a word that enables us to go on during sadness. Once students have unscrambled the word decision, direct them to find one phrase in chapter 7 (or think of one themselves) that shows how to make a decision for life, beginning with the letter in their hand. Samples: D-ear friends, do not be surprised that I have pain; E-xamine my feelings rather than let them control me; C-ontinue to do good; I-n tiny steps I'll make progress; S-ee the good that is continuing; I-'ll see the people God sends my way; O-thers get at least some of my time; N-othing God and I can't do.

8. Call for students to check off reasons they'll choose life under "Know You're Not Alone" in the space provided in chapter 7. Direct them to use these and other reasons to create a poster showing why they'll choose life. Ask: Why do people choose suicide? What other ways do people choose to die? Can you think of a time when death really would be better than life? How could we live on even in that circumstance? How does God's love motivate us to choose life rather than death? Invite all students to sign the poster and to circle each signature with every other student's initials as a commitment to choose life and help each other choose life. Guide the group to express support for each other by standing behind each student and inviting the group to bombard him/her with the reasons he/she is valuable and why they need him/her.

9. Invite a volunteer to read 2 Corinthians 1:3–5 and invite the group to share actions friends have done to help them through rough times. Point out the idea starters under "Help Someone Else Go On" in chapter 7. Guide the group to compose a pledge of commitment.

10. Explain that once we've been through shock, sadness, guilt and regret, anger, depression, questions, and the decision to go on with life, we're ready to live that decision. Ask: Will this happen instantly? (Not usually.) How can we bal-

ance moving on with remembering? Regret with future change?

Explain that after we've done our grief work, we're ready to give tribute, to remember in meaningful ways. Guide students to remember someone specific by completing one remembering action on pages 153–57 of chapter 8. Provide paper and other suggested materials. As they share ask: Why is this remembering meaningful to you? How does it help you live? Why are you glad this person was, or still is, a part of your life? How do you want to be remembered? How will you live your life to help this happen?

11. Guide students to repent a past mistake and make positive changes in light of it by overviewing Psalm 32 as guided by chapter 8. Explain that sad experiences invite not only a review of the past but a commitment to the present and future. Invite students to share what they think God wants their life to be like now that they've been through this death, diagnosis, disability, disappointment, or other rough time.

12. Distribute credit-card-sized poster board and direct students to write the words of Revelation 21:4 on it. Suggest they decorate it with a border and write on the back why they're willing to bank on this promise.